THE SOCIALIST PATRIOT

THE SOCIALIST PATRIOT

George Orwell and War

PETER STANSKY

stanford briefs
An Imprint of Stanford University Press
Stanford, California

Stanford University Press
Stanford, California

Printed in the United States of America
on acid-free, archival-quality paper

Library of Congress Cataloging-in-Publication Data

Names: Stansky, Peter, 1932– author.
Title: The socialist patriot : George Orwell and war / Peter Stansky.
Description: Stanford, California : Stanford Briefs, an imprint of
    Stanford University Press, 2023.
Identifiers: LCCN 2022043689 (print) | LCCN 2022043690 (ebook)
    | ISBN 9781503635494 (paperback) | ISBN 9781503635746 (ebook)
Subjects: LCSH: Orwell, George, 1903–1950—Political and social
    views. | Orwell, George, 1903–1950—Criticism, interpretation, etc.
    | War and literature—Great Britain--History—20th century.
Classification: LCC PR6029.R8 S73 2023 (print) | LCC PR6029.R8
    (ebook) | DDC 813/.6—dc23
LC record available at https://lccn.loc.gov/2022043689
LC ebook record available at https://lccn.loc.gov/2022043690

Cover design: Kevin Barrett Kane

Cover photo: Alamy, Editorial Royalty Free. Statue of George
Orwell by Martin Jennings, outside the BBC New Broadcasting
House.

Typeset by Classic Typography in 11/15 Adobe Garamond

CONTENTS

TO JOE AND ROBIN

Mr. Orwell is a revolutionary who is in love with 1910.

—Cyril Connolly reviewing *Animal Farm* in *Horizon*

September 1945

Writing about George Orwell:
An Autobiographical Introduction

In this study my intention is to discuss how and why George Orwell not only participated in but was also deeply influenced and shaped by the wars that he was involved in during his lifetime: the First World War, the Spanish Civil War, the Second World War, and the beginnings of the Cold War. But before doing so, as a preface it might be useful to account how it came about that I've been writing and thinking about George Orwell for more than seventy years, longer than Orwell's sadly short life.

It began some months before he died in January 1950, aged only forty-six. I read *Nineteen Eighty-Four* when it was first published in my senior year in high school, as a selection of the Book-of-the-Month Club to which my parents belonged. When growing up I also had an interest in the Spanish Civil War, sparked by my love of an album of its songs performed, if I remember correctly, by a chorus made up of German volunteers in the International Brigade.

The next step in my education was going to Yale where I became a history major, particularly interested in the history of Britain. I was fascinated by how British politics, society, culture, and the arts could mesh. In their own characteristic way they combined the ideological and the personal. This was reinforced by the generally Anglophile atmosphere at Yale. Although I was in no way involved with it, this was exemplified by the great publication project there of the letters of Horace Walpole. I became friends of graduate students who worked on that series. I was also much influenced by my classmate Russell Thomas, a nephew of the famous American editor, Maxwell Perkins, who seemed to be full of British literary gossip which we exchanged with others in our juvenile way over cups of tea in the Elizabethan Club or in a boozier fashion fueled by too much cheap sherry. There was also a lovely coincidence (I've always had a fascination with serendipity, a word invented by Horace Walpole). Bernard Knox, the teacher of a fantastic course on the Greek plays, had fought with the Loyalists in the Spanish Civil War. Also, I took an excellent seminar in my junior year taught by Leonard Krieger for those who were doing honors work in history. I'm not sure how it came about, but I wrote for it a paper on John Cornford who had fought and died in Spain, the great-grandson of Charles Darwin and son of the distinguished classicist Francis Cornford and his wife the poet Frances Cornford. It was also the occasion for my one slight brush with the McCarthyism of the period. In my paper I mentioned that Bernard Knox had been a military comrade of Cornford's in Spain. It was no secret as he had written about this experience in the memorial volume published after Cornford's death. Professor Krieger, who would be the only one who would see the paper, suggested that it was unwise to mention Bernard Knox in it as it might somehow get him in trouble in those 1950s Red Scare days.

My senior year would be largely devoted to writing my senior essay. I can't quite remember how my topic evolved, but it was about four Englishmen and how they were involved in the Spanish Civil War: John Cornford, Julian Bell, Stephen Spender, and George Orwell. It was not expected that such a work would be based on archival sources. As undergraduates in those days, we wouldn't travel for our research. In any case at that time hardly any primary material was available for any of these individuals. But there were sufficient printed sources for the purposes of my project. There was the Cornford memorial volume, and I spoke to Bernard Knox. Following Professor Krieger's advice I did not mention him in my work. Even some years later he didn't want to be identified by name as having fought in Spain. But eventually he published a series of excellent essays about the war. In one of them he mentioned that a Yale undergraduate had once exclaimed to him with excitement: "You're my thesis!" It must have been me. Stephen Spender had published in 1951 his memoir, *World Within World*. He had not fought in the war but had been closely involved in it. Julian Bell, the son of Vanessa Bell and the nephew of Virginia Woolf, had gone to Spain as an ambulance driver but had been killed when a bomb hit his vehicle. There was a memorial book about him, and in the early 1950s the ever growing interest in Bloomsbury was beginning. Most important George Orwell's *Homage to Catalonia* had been reissued in 1952 just as I was embarking on my senior essay. It had not sold well when it had been originally published in 1938 as the Right, by definition, didn't like it, and it also went against the then dominant Left interpretation of the war, much influenced by the Communist position. It is a brilliant and wonderful book, but its late success was helped by the Cold War. It was legitimately one of the Cold War's weapons because of its intense anti-Communism based on the Russian undermining of the cause of the Republic in Spain. In my senior essay I wanted to assess the significance of these four men, their backgrounds, and how and why they were involved in the Spanish Civil War. To do so I found myself increasingly committed to that exploration and much enjoying finding out as much as I could about their life stories leading up to their going to Spain. Cornford and Bell had died in Spain; their lives were cut tragically short at a young age, Cornford at twenty-one, Bell at twenty-nine.

Orwell had died at forty-six in January 1950. Spender was still alive, and some years later I would meet him. Orwell had become world famous with the publication of *Animal Farm* and *Nineteen Eighty-Four,* but the considerable Orwell literature and the systematic publication of his work had hardly begun. In fact that provided part of the fun of my research as I found it quite enjoyable to be able to wander the stacks of the Yale Library and track down the relevant fugitive Orwell publications in various periodicals. My very first publication, other than columns I wrote for the *Yale Daily News*, was in the *Yale Literary Magazine* in March, 1953: "The Tragedy of George Orwell: A Biographical Note." Though there were some errors and I would no longer agree with some of my interpretations, it reads fairly well so many years later.

What to do next with my life? I couldn't decide whether to go to law school or graduate school in history, so I decided to do neither and instead did a second BA in history at King's College Cambridge—the Bloomsbury college. Although I did not do any work on Bloomsbury then, that was one of the reasons I wished to go there. One had the pleasure of having E. M. Forster living in the college and frequently having lunch with undergraduates. And also by chance I became a member of a group who met fairly frequently at the home of Frances Cornford to have earnest discussions presided over by the wonderful Mrs. Cornford. I can't remember if I told her that I had written about her son, but in any case we didn't have any discussion about him. After Cambridge I thought I would go into publishing, but probably fortunately I did not find a decent job and I decided to do a PhD in history, a decision I have never regretted. I wrote a political thesis, subsequently published, on the British Liberal Party towards the end of the nineteenth century and the question of who would lead it after William Gladstone. One aspect of the history of the party at the time was the question of who would succeed Alfred Tennyson as poet laureate, but that material would not fit into my dissertation. At this point I met William Abrahams, poet, novelist, editor. I told him about that material and that resulted in my first academic publication, a joint article by us on the poet laureate issue published in *History Today*. Doing that had gone so well that he asked what we might write together next, and I showed him my senior essay on the four Englishmen and Spain. We went forward with that idea, secured a publishing contract, and embarked on the work. We did research on all four men. It became apparent that the four would not fit together easily, and so we decided to write a book about the two who had died in Spain, Cornford and Bell, with full cooperation and essential help by their families, although they were not authorized biographies. That was published in 1966 as *Journey to the Frontier*. Although we had cordial meetings with Stephen Spender, we decided not to write about him as he clearly wanted us to be discreet about the homosexual side of his life. A major part of his involvement with Spain was the difficult task of enabling his lover to leave the International Brigade. That meant we wouldn't go forward with that part of the project. Orwell, who had gone on to a much better known career after Spain, was obviously different from the other three.

To begin with, we did primary research on Cornford, Bell, and Orwell. We were in touch with the many still surviving relevant figures in their lives. For Orwell the two most important were his literary executor, Sir Richard Rees, and his executor, his widow Sonia Brownell Orwell. Rees provided the impetus for what turned out

to be our first Orwell book, *The Unknown Orwell*, published in 1972. He said to understand Orwell we needed
to find out more about Eric Blair before he adopted his
nom de plume (he never legally changed his name from
Eric Arthur Blair). *The Unknown Orwell* ended with the
first use in 1933 of his writing name George Orwell as the
author of his first book *Down and Out in Paris and London*. Rees also said that we shouldn't take too seriously
Orwell's wish in his will that there not be a biography of
him. In any case we never intended to write about his
total life but just about him through the Spanish Civil
War, our original conception. Our termination would be
the Spanish experience and what led up to it in his work
and life.

Our research in the early 1960s went very well. We
spoke to quite a few who had known him over the years.
Cyril Connolly who had been with him at his prep
school, St. Cyprian's, and his public school, Eton, was
very helpful as I recount in the text that follows, and we
were in touch with other Eton contemporaries. Through
the India office we established contact with those who
were with him in the police in Burma. We had cordial
meetings with Sonia Orwell who was very encouraging
and urged us to be in touch with Orwell's sister, Avril,
whom we visited in Scotland. At that point Sonia didn't
seem that interested in her late husband. The Orwell
Archive had been established at University College, London. It did not contain then much primary manuscript
material but was very useful as it had gathered together
his many publications in various periodicals. As neither

the four-volume *Collected Essays, Journalism and Letters* (1968) nor the twenty-volume *George Orwell: The Complete Works* (1986, 1987, 1998) had been published yet, it was immensely useful to have so many of the pieces printed in so many periodicals available in one place. Although our work would obviously have biographical aspects, it was not a biography, particularly as it would stop after Spain. Sonia Orwell raised no objection at that point.

But then disaster struck after the publication of *Journey to the Frontier* in 1966. Sonia Orwell had always had a troubled relation with Orwell's late request that there not be a biography of him. The biographical question was now much more on her mind, and she was much more involved with the Orwell world. He had become increasingly well-known after the publication of *Animal Farm,* and his fame and the money his estate was earning was continuing to grow in the years after his death. At some point she did appoint his friend Malcolm Muggeridge to write a biography of him. It might have been that she knew he would never do it, and hence it was a way of putting off quite a few other aspirant biographers. There had been the possibility of other biographers selected with her approval, most notably Richard Ellmann, but he ultimately declined. When we were in touch with her, ready to go forward with writing about Orwell after the publication of *Journey to the Frontier*, she said that clearly our intent was biographical. At that point we had not committed ourselves to what approach we would take. She said we could only go ahead with her permission if she could read what we'd written and have the power of totally controlling what we might publish. That was clearly unacceptable, so we determined to proceed on our own and as we thought best. We were banned from the Archive but we had done research in it earlier, and it still didn't have, as it does now, much original material. And there were quite a bit of primary sources available elsewhere. We also had material in the form of documents and verbal and written reminiscences from those who had known him. As Sonia had a mixed reputation among quite a few of these individuals, her disapproval was unlikely to affect their relationship with us. Ultimately lawyers read the manuscript of our two Orwell books and made sure that we did not use quotations beyond what would be acceptable through the policy of fair usage, that is, we would not violate copyright restrictions. We were reprimanded by Orwell's agent, Mark Hamilton, for quoting two very short complete works of art, Orwell's first two publications in a local newspaper, his intensely patriotic short poems written as a schoolboy during the First World War. Ironically we had unearthed them. He said he would refrain from taking legal steps against us. Such action might have led to legal expenses, but it would also have given the book a fair amount of publicity.

The Unknown Orwell, published in 1972, received a lot of attention, most of it highly favorable including a fine review by Cyril Connolly. It and its successor, *Orwell: The Transformation*, published in 1979, both made the short list for the American National Book Award. Sonia published a letter saying our first book was full of errors, and she would make them known but she never did so. In reaction to that book she appointed Bernard Crick to write Orwell's biography. When it was finished she tried to prevent its publication. He had an ironclad guarantee for publication so her efforts were unsuccessful. In effect we unlocked the Orwell biography logjam. There have now been quite a few excellent biographies with more to come as well as innumerable studies of him. Reading Orwell, thinking about him, writing about him, has been a major part of my life ever since I read *Nineteen Eighty-Four* in 1949.

THE SOCIALIST PATRIOT

1 BEFORE THE FIRST WORLD WAR

More than seventy years after his death on January 21, 1950, George Orwell is more alive in our minds than he may have been in his lifetime. There are several obvious reasons for this. With the never-ending explosion of technology, the world has become more "Orwellian" in its dominant negative sense. Those who wish to know more about us than we may choose are now able to do so more easily than ever before: governments, businesses anxious to sell us something, intrusive individuals or agencies, governmental and otherwise, for possibly benign or possibly nefarious reasons. It's not quite the telescreen of *Nineteen Eighty-Four* but it is close. Our actions on our computers can be so easily tracked and traced. Also, Donald Trump did wonders for the sales of *Nineteen Eighty-Four* and other works by Orwell through his popularization, so to speak, of the ideas of "alternative facts" and "fake news." Here was the work of Winston Smith at the Ministry of Truth come to life.

I wish to examine here the ways in which war shaped Orwell's life, writings, and thinking. William Abrahams and I in our *Orwell: The Transformation* (1979) argued, looking at his life from the publication of *Down and Out in Paris and London* in 1933 through his experiences in the Spanish Civil War, that his fighting on behalf of the Republic in Spain led him finally to commit fully to his own version of being a democratic socialist. This book considers two important aspects of Orwell's life: his relation to war and his feelings about his country. There are interesting contradictions and paradoxes in his thoughts about these two questions. To a considerable extent they can be examined and explained through his reactions to the wars he experienced. I believe that the most important war in shaping him as the writer and person he became was the First World War when he was quite young, taking place during his adolescence from his eleventh to his fourteenth year. It has been the most neglected war in the assessments of his life and work. I will also be considering the other wars he experienced: the Spanish Civil War, the Second World War, and the early years of the Cold War. *Animal Farm* and *Nineteen Eighty-Four* are crucial Cold War documents, among other things. The *Oxford English Dictionary* cites him as the first coiner of the term *cold war* in his column in *Tribune* on October 19, 1945. Nor, although it played a crucial role in how he experienced the First World War, has enough attention been devoted, I believe, to the importance of his class position in determining his attitudes and ideas. He famously described himself, with wonderful precision, as a member of the "lower-upper-middle class" which he defined as being part of the upper middle class but without money. As we know from the extensive ramifications of class in England, money can play an extremely important role in the establishment of a family. But perhaps more than in other societies one can remain part of the upper middle classes, even if in its lower rungs, based on one's family even if one isn't particularly well off. It is more of a challenge but it is doable. One could also remain part of what might be called the "official" classes despite one's comparative lack of income, based on one's family's inheritance and position. Such was indubitably the case with George Orwell, as the son of a civil servant and as an official in the Empire for five years when he served as a police officer in Burma. This is somewhat contrary to the position he took about the ruling role of money in his novel *Keep the Aspidistra Flying*.

Orwell was a deeply patriotic socialist, shaped significantly by his growing up before and during the First World War. On the face of it patriot and socialist are not concepts that one might normally link. Some might think that they are somewhat contradictory terms. On the other hand, that combination was not all that uncommon in England. In many ways Orwell was a traditional Englishman harboring quite a few easy prejudices against Jews, homosexuals, and women. At the same time, perhaps paradoxically, he was a profound and powerful believer in and advocate of human decency. As he pointed out himself, he never could carry out in action these prejudices against particular individuals. He was very fond of quite a few members of all those groups although he never fell into the cliché "some of my best friends are . . ." He did have Jewish and queer friends and had a very happy marriage as well as quite a few affairs. His belief and nostalgia for what might be called traditional Englishness can be found particularly in the novel *Coming Up for Air*, written just before the Second World War with its evocation, even when approached with some irony, of a bucolic First World War England. Most powerfully his commitment to socialism and patriotism can be seen in the two very short works he wrote during the Second World War, *The Lion and the Unicorn* and *The English People*. In the latter he evoked a decent and in many ways traditional concept of what he thought England was like. At the same time in *The Lion and the Unicorn,* with its subtitle *Socialism and the English Genius,* he called for a revolutionary transformation of the country into a socialist state by revolution if necessary. The lion and the unicorn are the heraldic beasts that support the royal coat of arms. The subtitle conveys the idea that socialism could and should come about in England. In this he was very much in one English tradition, a striking combination of traditional and radical values. Think of William Blake calling for the building of Jerusalem in England's green and pleasant land. Think of William Cobbett celebrating rural England, holding many reac-

tionary views, yet at the same time being a radical journalist demanding democratic political reform. Think of
the Marxist William Morris glorifying an older England
of medieval guilds yet believing firmly that there needed
to be a revolution to bring about a totally socialist society. Orwell was a unique thinker at the same time that he
was in a very important English tradition. In a sense he
made this tradition global in his lashing out in *Animal
Farm* and *Nineteen Eighty-Four* against totalitarianism as
it might be found anywhere but particularly in the Soviet
Union.

George Orwell was a created name, a pseudonym,
almost rather casually selected as his writing name for his
first book, *Down and Out in Paris and London*. He had
mixed feelings about the Scottishness of his given first
name, Eric. He also hated intensely the association of that
name with the mawkish famous public school novel of
1858 by Dean Farrar, *Eric, or Little by Little*. He sent four
possibilities to his publisher Victor Gollancz: H. Lewis
Allways, P. C. Burton, Kenneth Miles, and George Orwell.
He had a slight preference for the last, George, that most
English of names, and Orwell, the Suffolk river near
where his parents lived. But he left the final choice to his
publisher. Hence George Orwell was born. Also he did
want to avoid any possible embarrassment to his parents
over the account of his poverty-stricken life in Paris and
as a tramp in England. I will generally call him Orwell
in this study although he did not as a writer exclusively

use George Orwell rather than Eric Blair until after the Spanish Civil War. And he was known as George Orwell to most of those he came to know after the war.

He was born (and later buried) as Eric Arthur Blair on June 25, 1903, in Motihari, Bengal, where his father Richard Walmesley Blair was a subdeputy agent of the Opium Department of the Indian Civil Service. His mother, Ida Limouzin Blair, was a bit exotic as her father was French although her mother was English, and she had many relations in the Indian Civil Service. Ida was born in England, in Penge, Surrey, but spent much of her early life in Moulmein in Burma. There her father pursued his not very successful business interests, mostly in teak and tea. The town is now perhaps best known in English literature as where Orwell was forced to shoot an elephant.

Much of English life was and perhaps still is devoted to the significance of the ramifications of class. Very fine distinctions can be made, and it can be a consuming game and a significant one. Who are one's parents? Who are one's ancestors? Where did one grow up? Where did one go to primary and secondary school? This is generally more important than where one went to university, particularly as it was not until after the Second World War that going to university became more important for one's career and was more likely to be experienced by all members of the middle class. (Although it might be significant if one wanted to be a leading politician. Most but not all prime ministers of the nineteenth and twentieth centuries went to Oxford or Cambridge, and most of them

went to the grandest colleges there, Christ Church at
Oxford and Trinity at Cambridge. Of course there were
notable exceptions such as Winston Churchill and Benjamin Disraeli. But as the grandson of the Duke of Marlborough, Churchill was certainly extremely well born.)

Eric Arthur Blair was a member of the English establishment, born into it by descent, although by his time
he was at a fairly low level. In some accounts he has been
characterized as an outsider, but nothing I believe could
be further from the truth. He wrote from the inside of
English society at the same time that he was endowed
with a powerful ability to take that world apart and look
at it with a cold yet sympathetic eye. He knew it so well
based on his inheritance and his upbringing. His primary
and secondary schooling were at the highest levels, much
as he came to question his education. It helped train the
very literary skills that enabled him in his writings to
criticize it so effectively. Class discriminations were perhaps most important in the middle class where the finer
distinctions could be made, where the nuances of the significance of being, say, at a particular school could be
assessed. And in many ways they were most intense in the
years he was growing up. Class markers might well have
been more significant in the increasingly unstable world
of the first half of the twentieth century in comparison to
the years that had gone before. Yet those who were members of the aristocracy or the working class were far less
likely to need to worry to any serious extent about these
finer points. Indeed Orwell had some connection with

the aristocracy. It was very much in the past, but it was never forgotten by his family, memorialized in a few of the family mementos it retained and Orwell himself was quite fond of, particularly as he inherited some of them. His great-great-grandfather had been married to a daughter of the Earl of Westmorland, and her portrait was a treasured possession of Orwell's family and ultimately of his own. His grandfather had been an Anglican clergyman, a position generally of an assured class position but which might or might not have a substantial income. His grandfather did, but there wasn't enough to provide sufficient unearned income for his numerous children. Orwell's father was very much a younger son; he definitely needed to secure a respectable job that would support him and his family. Being a civil servant in India, even at a fairly low level, meant that he could afford to live there with a certain style and employ quite a few servants. There is a charming photo of the infant Eric with his Indian nurse.

Even so, six months after Eric's birth his mother, his sister Marjorie, five years older, and Eric himself went to live in England, quite a few years before his father retired in 1911 at the age of fifty-five. His early years could hardly have been spent in a more English location, both in Henley-on-Thames, site of the annual regatta, and then in its neighboring village of Shiplake during those golden, at least in retrospect, Edwardian days before the First World War. His father did come home once on leave for three months, fathering Orwell's younger sister, Avril. So Orwell hardly saw his father in his very early years. When he came home permanently Orwell was on his way to boarding school so would only be with his father during school holidays.

Orwell knew that he was part of the professional classes at the heart of England: in his words years later "soldiers, clergymen, government officials, teachers, lawyers, doctors, etc." (*The Complete Works of George Orwell,* ed. Peter Davison, vol. 19, London: Secker & Warburg, 1998, 86; hereafter referred to as CW followed by volume and page). It was a central group in English society for whom it was more important to be of some service to the state than to make a lot of money, although there was no objection to money should it appear in the process. By Orwell's time there was very little family money left. The wealthiest member of his family had been his great-great-grandfather Charles Blair. He had made a fortune in Jamaica, no doubt deeply involved with and profiting from slavery. He further established himself through his marriage to Lady Mary Fane, the second daughter of Thomas, the eighth Earl of Westmorland. The Fane family was not only aristocratic but had as well poets, composers, and playwrights in the family tree. The seventh Earl had been Chancellor of Oxford University and built Mereworth Castle, one of the finest Palladian buildings in England. (Near to it, Orwell would pick hops years later.) The eighth Earl was the godfather of Orwell's grandfather, the vicar. Orwell's father was the tenth child of a vicar who, even with a rich living, had little money to spare for his younger children. Hence Richard Blair had little choice but to make a living, in his case as a civil servant. But that did not mean that the class status the family's social position had conferred wouldn't still be part of Orwell's inheritance. It could help instill that innate sense of authority, one of Orwell's important attributes as a writer and thinker. In 1936 in a poem published in the *Adelphi* he stated that he might have been a happy vicar "two hundred years ago" in grim contrast to the present world, "an evil time" (CW 10, 524). By chance, perhaps Orwell had an enhanced sense of his status even when young. For the first eight years of his life he was the man of the house, although his mother, Ida, was a very strong-willed woman. He was fatherless most of the time except for the first months of his life and the short time when his father was home on leave.

In September 1911 Orwell went to St. Cyprian's, his prep school located at Eastbourne on the Sussex coast. He was admitted on half-fees as a bright boy who was likely to bring credit to the school by winning a scholarship to a grand public school. His family couldn't afford the full fees. It was probably also in his favor in the view of the imperially minded proprietors of the school that his father had served as a civil servant in India. The school was immortalized, not to its credit, by his bitter essay, "Such, Such Were the Joys," that he wrote about his school days many years later, probably in 1947. Its

title was a satirical use of a line by William Blake. Some
have thought he didn't mean for it to be published, but
he clearly did. He sent a copy of it to his publisher, Fredric Warburg, writing: "It is really too libelous to print,
and I am not disposed to change it, except perhaps the
names. But I think it should be printed sooner or later
when the people most concerned are dead" (CW 19, 149,
May 31, 1947). In it he claims that he was eventually told
that as his family was not paying full fees he was under
particular pressure to do well and win a scholarship at a
leading public school. St. Cyprian's played a crucial role
in shaping him as an accredited member of the lower-
upper-middle class. It was a comparatively new school,
having been founded in 1898 by Mr. and Mrs. Vaughan
Wilkes and had about eighty students. In many ways it
gave him a good education with its emphasis on the classics and the necessity to write well if he were to secure a
scholarship to a top-ranked public school.

And as much as he would resent the school, it almost
inevitably helped to instill in him an intense sense of
patriotism. These schools were designed to train those
who would rule the Empire and the state. The British
Empire, although challenged, was at this point the greatest in the world. There was little reason to think that
despite the rivalry of Germany and the United States it
would not remain so. In many ways it was a period where
a sense not only of the Empire but also of its problems
was at its height, the age of Kipling and Newbolt. But
the Boer War at the turn of the century had not been an

easy one and had challenged the hegemony of Britain. It had increased both a sense of anxiety about the Empire and criticism of it as well as an increased commitment to it. Particularly worrying were the number of potential recruits who were turned away as not physically fit. The Vaughan Wilkeses were intensely Empire minded. One of their sons would have a distinguished career in its service. Orwell would eventually become a strong anti-imperialist but not because he necessarily believed in the virtues of those whom the British ruled. Rather, in his ultimate view, the British had no right to rule other people. Similar to many supporters of the Empire he might well think that the native races were less capable of good government than were the British. But that did not entitle the British to be in control. Ultimately Orwell regarded imperialism as evil and felt that he needed to expiate his guilt for having participated in it.

2 THE FIRST WORLD WAR

Orwell's last two years at St. Cyprian's, 1914–1916, were the first two years of the First World War. Such schools' intense sense of loyalty to their country would be made even more so by the war. Yet, somewhat oddly, the war itself doesn't figure to any extent in his piece about the school, "Such, Such Were the Joys." He did publish in 1940, significantly the first year of the Second World War, a powerful essay about this time in his life: "My Country Right or Left." In it we find the young Blair being instilled with an intense sense of patriotism even before going to St. Cyprian's but not necessarily from the war itself. He does mention that he had a much more vivid memory of the sinking of the *Titanic* in 1912 than the Battle of the Marne during the war. In this essay he wrote: "Most of the English middle class are trained for war from the cradle onwards, not technically but morally. The earliest political slogan I can remember is 'We want eight (eight dreadnoughts [the most advanced battleships]) and we

13

won't wait.' At seven years old I was a member of the Navy League and wore a sailor suit with 'H.M.S. *Invincible*' on my cap. Even before my public-school O.T.C. [Officer Training Corps] I had been in a private-school cadet corps. On and off, I had been toting a rifle ever since I was ten" (CW 12, 270). He noted some years later, in 1945, how easy then it was to buy a rifle. "I bought my first Saloon Rifle at the age of 10, with no questions asked" (CW 17, 411). The school was particularly addicted to shooting, doing extremely well in national competitions, but there is no indication that Orwell participated in them. It is intriguing that in a short list he compiled in 1949 some months before his death he wrote that he didn't wish this brief essay, "My Country Right or Left," in which he made these points, reprinted (CW 20, 229). Why? He didn't indicate any reason. Did he not want it remembered that a rather simple-minded patriotism had been instilled in him when he was very young? Yet elsewhere he is not hesitant to indicate how fond he was of and committed to traditional English values despite his intense criticisms of English society. This would become vividly apparent at the time of the Second World War.

The First World War would be followed closely at the school, particularly on posted maps. Old Boys of the school would be in the armed forces, and their deaths were commemorated in the *St. Cyprian's Chronicle*. One hundred fifty-five served in the war and thirty-six were killed, a notable number considering that the school had only been founded recently. The feeling of the boys at the school might be made more complex as the war was unlikely to last long enough for them to serve. Would they miss what Christopher Isherwood called "the Test?" Would they somehow fail, through no fault of their own, to be patriotic enough? Much effort was devoted, at that impressionable age, to supporting the war effort: improbably knitting socks and mufflers for the troops and visiting recovering soldiers at a nearby military camp, handing out Woodbine cigarettes. The Cadet Corps formed an honor guard when the King and Queen visited the camp. The war would be ever present, making the school even more Spartan in the quality of the food and being even colder because of the lack of coal. At the time of the signing of the Russo-German pact in August 1939, these early experiences came home despite Orwell's having been a pacifist after his return from the Spanish Civil War. "I was patriotic at heart. . . . I knew . . . that the long drilling in patriotism which the middle classes go through had done its work" (CW 12, 271). He wrote in his diary on September 9, 1940, "I would give my life for England readily enough, if I thought it necessary" (CW 12, 229). And as he wrote about patriotism in his 1945 essay "Notes on Nationalism": "By 'patriotism' I mean devotion to a particular place and a particular way of life, which one believes to be the best in the world but has no wish to force upon other people. Patriotism is of its nature defensive, both militarily and culturally.

Nationalism, on the other hand, is inseparable from the desire for power" (CW 17, 142).

Two significant indications of his early sense of patriotism were the two poems he published while at the school: "Awake! Young Men of England" and "Kitchener." Possibly in the case of the second poem, written when he was older and somewhat more sophisticated, he might not have totally endorsed its sentiments and had written what was expected of him rather than what he actually felt. But I tend to think that he largely shared the views expressed. He had been a poet since the age of four or five when he dictated a poem to his mother about a tiger, perhaps inspired by William Blake's famous poem. He eventually wrote a fair number of poems and was always interested in poetry. Years later he would create an oral poetry "magazine," *Voice*, when he was at the BBC during the Second World War as well as doing seven broadcasts for the Eastern Service on contemporary British poetry. The well-known photograph of some of those he worked with on *Voice* at the BBC during the war included T. S. Eliot and William Empson.

He began his publication career, his very first appearance in print, with "Awake! Young Men of England," a deeply patriotic poem. It appeared in the *Henley and South Oxfordshire Standard* on October 2, 1914. His mother had sent the poem to the paper. The death of his first cousin, Neville Lascelles Ward, the son of his mother's sister, may well have inspired the poem. Second

Lieutenant Ward was a graduate of Sandhurst and a member of the East Surrey Regiment, which went to France as part of the British Expeditionary Force almost immediately after the outbreak of war. He was killed at the battle of Mons in Belgium on August 23. It was likely that Eric was home from school when the family heard the news. (See Peter Duby "The Man Who Inspired George Orwell's First Published Work," *Orwell Society Newsletter,* no. 4, June 2014.) The poem could hardly be more patriotic. The school learned of the poem, and the headmaster and his formidable wife were so impressed by it that Orwell was asked to read it aloud to the assembled boys. It would lead to a brief period when he would be "in favor" by Mrs. Vaughan Wilkes, a contrast to all the times he was in trouble with her, so painfully chronicled in his memoir of his time there.

I feel a special connection with the poem. On the basis of a lead provided by Ian Angus, at that point curator of the Orwell collection at University College, William Abrahams and I in the course of our Orwell research many years ago were, I believe, the first to unearth this very first publication as well as the subsequent patriotic poem, his second appearance in print. The intense and rather primitive patriotism—very different from jingoism—that inspired "Awake! Young Men of England" was to provide an essential and ineradicable part of his character, even as it became more sophisticated. The poem was as follows:

Oh! give me the strength of the lion,
  The wisdom of Reynard the fox,
And then I'll hurl troops at the Germans,
  And give them the hardest of knocks.

Oh! think of the War lord's mailed fist,
  That is striking at England to-day;
And think of the lives of our soldiers
  Are fearlessly throwing away.

Awake! oh you young men of England,
  For if, when your Country's in need
You do not enlist by the thousand,
  You truly are cowards indeed. (CW 10, 20)

His second publication, again a poem, "Kitchener," was also connected with the war. It too was published in the *Henley and South Oxfordshire Standard* on July 21, 1916, sent in by the author himself. He had written it when the boys at the school had been asked to commemorate Lord Kitchener's death in either prose or verse. His first poem had appeared with its author given as Master Eric Blair. The second was by the more grown-up E. A. Blair. Lord Kitchener, the Secretary of State for War, had died on June 5. The ship that was carrying him to Russia on a mission struck a German mine. A very popular and famous figure, he had had an extremely distinguished military career: the victor in the battle of Omdurman in 1898 that established British control of the Sudan and revenged the death of General Gordon some years before.

He was then, in British eyes, a hero of the Boer War in South Africa. Yet he was not an effective War Secretary though he was in many ways central for the war effort. A poster of his recognizable face and pointed finger became the most famous poster of the war, designed by Alfred Leete. Its text read in two versions either "Your country needs YOU" or "BRITONS want YOU." In the first two years of the war there was no conscription of young men although many volunteered to serve, in part inspired by the poster. The young Blair wrote:

No stone is set to mark his nation's loss,
No stately tomb enshrines his noble breast,
Not e'en the tribute of a wooden cross
        Can mark this hero's rest.

He needs them not; his name ungarnished stands
Remindful of the mighty deeds he worked,
Footprints of one, upon time's changeful sands,
        Who n'er his duty shirked.

Who follows in his steps no danger shuns,
Nor stoops to conquer by a shameful deed,
As honest and unselfish race he runs,
        From fear and malice freed. (CW 10, 20)

The sophistication of the now thirteen-year-old is vividly conveyed in his comments on the Kitchener poem that had been written by his school mate Cyril Connolly. "*Dashed* good. Slight repetition. Scansion excellent. Meaning a little ambiguous in places. Epithets for the most part well selected. The whole thing is neat, elegant, and polished" (CW 10, 21). Connolly's poem is more elegiac and romantic than Orwell's more straightforwardly patriotic effort. Of course we don't know how deeply Orwell held the values enunciated in the poem, but it would be reasonable to think that he had been shaped by the patriotic ideas of the time that the school was so dedicated to imbue. The poem instructed one never to shirk one's duty, to be brave and honorable, honest and unselfish, and free from cowardice and malice. Mrs. Vaughan Wilkes proudly pasted the published poem in her scrap book, presumably given to her by Eric or sent to her by his family. Contrary to what he wrote, as was here often the case, he was because of it very much in her favor, a constant concern of the boys. His exalted status was for not only having written the poem, but he had also just won a scholarship to Wellington, the preeminent public school with military ties. It may not have been until he was a bit older that he began to have doubts about the greatness of Britain. As he remarked to Connolly when they were both at Eton, Britain would emerge from the First World War a second-class nation. But that would not necessarily diminish his affection and appreciation for his native land, despite his many reservations and disapprovals.

He wrote "Such, Such Were the Joys" in the 1940s about his days at St. Cyprian's. For reasons of libel, it couldn't be published in England until 1968 when Mrs. Vaughan Wilkes was dead, though it was published in the United States in 1952 in the *Partisan Review*. It is a very bleak picture of the school. Orwell's view of the school was publicly supported by some of its graduates and attacked by others. The writing of the piece had been stimulated by Cyril Connolly, his friend there and at Eton, who wrote about the school in his *Enemies of Promise* (1938). There it had also been depicted negatively, although later Connolly came to revise his opinion and think more favorably about the school and the concern that the Vaughan Wilkeses had for his education. Several have cited the fact that he attended Mrs. Vaughan Wilkes's funeral as evidence for this, but he actually told William Abrahams and myself that he went to it to be sure that she was dead. On the other hand, when we had visited him some time before, it was he who told us that she was then still alive, lived close by, and that we must go to see her. Our visit was indeed extremely interesting and useful. She emphasized how much in her view she had tried to reach out to the young Orwell. As far as I can remember she did not mention his essay, although it was likely she knew about it. She certainly knew about Orwell's view of the school and that he was unhappy there. I presume we thought it would be tactless to mention it. But he was the school's most famous graduate, exceeding the reputation of Cecil Beaton, Cyril Connolly, and Gavin Maxwell. We had asked Connolly whether he had been to see her while she was still alive, but he said of course not, he would have been too scared.

Orwell's letters home rather routinely said how well everything was going, but they may have been written under the supervision of the staff. In any case he was unlikely to share his unhappiness with his family. As I've said, it's somewhat odd that the war is not mentioned in his memoir. It begins famously with his writing that shortly after he arrived at the school, at the age of eight, he started to wet his bed and that he was severely punished for it. It turns out that this was probably untrue. Orwell was using the experience of another boy to make dramatic through fiction a truthful and valid point about the school, what he saw as its brutality (see citations CW 19, 356). He wrote about the paradox at the heart of all such schools at the time:

> The essential conflict was between the tradition of nineteenth-century asceticism and the actually existing luxury and snobbery of the pre-1914 age. On the one side were low-church Bible Christianity, sex puritanism, insistence on hard work, respect for academic achievement, disapproval of self-indulgence: on the other, contempt for "braininess" and worship of games, contempt for foreigners and the working class, an almost neurotic dread of poverty, and, above all, the assumption not only that money and privilege are the things that matter, but that is better to inherit them than to have to work for them. Broadly, you were bidden to be at once a Christian and a social success, which is impossible. (CW 19, 375)

He exaggerated his own sense of his failure. "I was damned, I had no money, I was weak, I was ugly, I was unpopular, I had a chronic cough, I was cowardly, I smelt" (CW 19, 379). What is important, I believe, is that, for better or worse, the values of the class he was born into, "upper-lower-middle class," were further taught and beaten into him at his prep school. In so many ways, criticize them as he might, they remained with him for the rest of his life. By descent and education he had been trained to serve and value the state. Deeply question it as he would, its values were still an important part of who he was. He was a patriot.

In many ways it was a good education. The requisite work in Greek and Latin, the writing of essays, helped this very intelligent boy to become a writer. It also helped his immediate career. He had been taken on half-fees on the assumption that he would win a scholarship—awarded on merit, not need—to a prominent public school. He did win the Harrow History Prize but apparently did not try to enter Harrow although St. Cyprian's had a special relationship with that school. He sat the entrance examinations for Wellington and also spent two and a half grueling days of written and oral exams at Eton. He succeeded at Wellington and entered that school, which he hated, in January 1917. He had placed fourteenth on the scholarship list at Eton, no mean feat, but there were only thirteen openings. But then, fortunately, another place became available, and he entered Eton as a King's Scholar. A senior King's Scholar had left, probably to enlist. He would live in college as a member of an academic elite of seventy. They might be somewhat looked down upon as "tugs" by the approximately nine hundred other boys who paid full fees, the so-called Oppidans, but they probably felt superior to them. They were the heart of Henry VI's foundation. Eton was the most famous English public school, and Orwell would be irretrievably in later life an Old Etonian and was recognized as such. That remained true no matter that in 1947 he characterized it as "the most costly and snobbish of the English Public Schools. But I had only got in there by the means of a scholarship; otherwise my father could not have afforded to send me to a school of this type" (CW 19, 86). He had, however, a quite undistinguished academic career there. He had worked very hard to secure the position, and then he rather slacked off. That does not mean that he was intellectually inactive, but he did not pay as much attention to his formal studies as he should have, although he had a rich and wide range of reading and interests. Yet his career at Eton had some moderate successes: he gave a recitation from Robert Louis Stevenson to parents and Old Etonians at one of the most important events of the year, the annual celebration of the birthday of George III, the Fourth of June. He scored a rare goal in a practice game at the arcane Eton sport played by his fellow King's Scholars: the Wall Game. He was elected to College Pop. Yet when he left, he didn't go to Oxford or Cambridge unlike virtually all the King's Scholars. There is quite a debate about that issue and to what degree he wanted to and whether or not it would have been possible. His tutor, the classicist, A.S.F. Gow, advised against it and his father agreed. Gow recognized him as a bright boy but one who had nevertheless not distinguished himself in his studies and in his view would have been incapable of securing the necessary scholarship at one of the "ancient universities." Orwell himself may not have been particularly interested in going on to university, although Jacintha Buddicom, the girl he was in love with at home, thought otherwise, and she believed that his mother supported the idea. His contemporary in college, Steven Runciman, thought he rather wanted to go East, to Burma. In any case Gow and his father agreed that that was what he should do, and he took the requisite exams to qualify for an appointment as an officer in the Burma Police force.

He had received a good education at Eton both in his classes and tutorials and through his extensive reading of Shaw, Chesterton, Wells, and Butler, authors he had been interested in ever since St. Cyprian's. A new great enthusiasm at Eton was A. E. Housman. He knew by heart virtually all the verses of *A Shropshire Lad*. Housman was a friend of Gow's and came to visit and gave a talk at Eton. Orwell had an assignment to put two of his verses into Latin. His poetry, though full too of despair, would reinforce an idealization of rural England. It might be a country that deserved to be fought for. As he wrote in his essay "Inside the Whale" years later, Housman's poems were full of "the charm of buried villages, the nostalgia of place-names . . . thatched roofs and the jingle of smithies, the wild jonquils in the pastures." Housman was the perfect poet for the adolescent Etonian, nostalgic but also cynical and sad. As Orwell wrote: "He was patriotic, it was true, but in a harmless old-fashioned way, to the

tune of red coats and 'God Save the Queen' rather than
steel helmets and 'Hang the Kaiser.' And he was satisfy-
ingly anti-Christian—he stood for a kind of bitter, defi-
ant paganism, a conviction that life is short and the gods
are against you, which exactly fitted the prevailing mood
of the young; and all in the charming fragile verse that
was composed almost entirely of words of one syllable"
(CW 12, 93–95). At the same time he saw Housman as a
repudiation of the official beliefs and conventions of the
age. Housman particularly appealed to adolescents, and
Orwell might have been more sentimental than he was
willing to admit. Years later after Burma when he visited
Gow, then a Fellow at Trinity College, Cambridge, he
met Housman at dinner at the college's High Table. It is
true that paying for Oxford or Cambridge might have
been a considerable challenge, but one suspects that
money might have been found at one of the colleges for
an Etonian King's Scholar. But instead, as did many
other Etonians, particularly the Oppidans, he entered the
family business, in his case becoming an officer in the
police in Burma, although the Indian Imperial Police was
not a very distinguished part of the Empire. His projected career would be very similar to his father's.

  He went to Eton in May 1917, a month before his
fourteenth birthday. The war had a little more than a year
to go. Ultimately 5,687 Old Etonians would serve in the
war; 1,160 were killed (67 of them King's Scholars), and
1,467 were wounded. The names of the dead would be
read out in chapel and, as in many other schools, ulti-

mately immortalized with their names carved into the walls. Although the war would not last long enough for Orwell to be conscripted, many known to those at the school were in the military services. No doubt virtually all those who would leave school in the first year and a half that he was there would become officers. Some left early in order to serve. So indeed it happened in Orwell's case that with such a departure a place became open for him to occupy in the Election of 1916, as the total num ber of King's Scholars was strictly limited. It's hard to believe that there was not a strong atmosphere in the school of the importance of serving the state during the war in a military capacity. The war made it possible for him to attend Eton. Although the war was followed closely on posted maps, it did not much affect day to day life, other than the bad food. Orwell claimed that his chief memory of the war years at Eton was having to use margarine rather than butter.

Yet no school in Britain was more strongly attached to the powers that be and provided and continues to provide many prime ministers, most recently David Cameron and Boris Johnson. The King's Scholars were a very bright group of sophisticated adolescents, and not surprisingly a fair number of them were likely to have a high degree of cheeky cynicism, prone to questioning the values that the school existed to inculcate. These were very bright youngsters who would enjoy arguing with one another. Contrary to what some have said, Orwell fully participated in the life of college although some noted that he had a certain air of aloofness. He did rather enjoy, as he would for the rest of life, challenging even then conventional values. One of his contemporaries even compared him to Socrates in his ability to question the beliefs of his colleagues, which his fellow Etonians were to some degree taken aback by. He became known as being outspoken and cynical. One contemporary remarked that he was the first person he knew who would make critical remarks about his parents. The war led to the questioning of traditional values among these bright young men: Shouldn't a better and different world emerge after the war? They felt, as Etonians, they were likely to have and were entitled to successful careers. He probably realized, however, that with his comparatively modest background and his lack of scholarly achievement he might have a less distinguished future. Yet whatever he might be thinking, whatever his public remarks might be, his sense that he was obligated to support his country, particularly at the time of war, was reinforced at Eton, no matter how much he might discount it both while he was there and afterwards. He also profited, despite his lack of academic success, from its perhaps surprisingly undoctrinaire education. In his future life his career would be helped, as undoubtedly it was for many other Old Etonians, by his Eton connections. In his case it was Cyril Connolly, Richard Rees, John Lehmann, L. H. Myers, and David Astor, even if they hadn't been there at the same time. Orwell felt at times that he did not quite have the class status of those who were at Eton.

I think that this was more wishful thinking, his unsuccessful occasional attempts during his lifetime to identify with a lower class than his own. Perhaps he was at the very lowest social level of those who were at Eton. But through family and education he fit in. He was not particularly gregarious there and few felt they knew him well. That was more his choice than otherwise. But unlike St. Cyprian's, his time there was comparatively happy and fruitful, despite his lack of academic distinction.

Loyal to his family commitment to service to the state, Orwell's father, unnecessarily as he was sixty, enlisted in 1917 and became possibly the oldest second lieutenant in the British army, looking after mules at an army camp outside of Marseilles. Orwell's mother and older sister, Marjorie, moved to London. Mrs. Blair went to work for the Ministry of Pensions, and Marjorie as a dispatch rider for the Women's Legion which assisted the war effort both at home and in France. His younger sister, Avril, was placed in a boarding school in Ealing. The Blair family was clearly doing its bit. However cheeky he might be, Orwell had no choice but to be in the Officer Training Corps at Eton. It had been established comparatively recently there, and the war put an increased emphasis on its importance. It would supply the young officers who were the most likely to die at the front. The school had recommitted to the war the previous year when the headmaster, Edward Lyttelton, had been forced out in 1916 because of his remark that he did not believe that the

Germans were beasts. As Christopher Hollis, an older contemporary of Orwell's at college, wrote in his history of the school: "Patriotism and the readiness to sacrifice one's life for one's country had been the quality to which Eton had paid especial—and what to its critics might appear exaggerated—honour." (Hollis, *Eton: A History*, London: Hollis and Carter, 1970, 297–298). As Orwell said years later to his friend Richard Rees, "his generation must be marked forever by the humiliation of not having taken part" in the First World War. (Rees, *George Orwell: Fugitive from the Camp of Victory*, London: Secker & Warburg, 1961, 154). He certainly liked Eton much more than St. Cyprian's and made good friends there, even though he tended to be rather aloof and distant. Years later, in 1948, he wrote a brief review of a book about Eton without any indication that he had gone there. He predicted inaccurately that it was "a form of education that is hardly likely to last much longer. . . . It is almost impossible that Eton should survive in anything like its present form." He underestimated the extraordinary ability of such English institutions to adapt and hence be able to maintain their core nature to a great degree, surprisingly unchanged. Eton still flourishes, far less different than one might expect. In the review he did extol what was good about the school presumably based on his own experience: that it has "a tolerant and civilised atmosphere which gives each boy a fair chance of developing his own individuality" (*The Observer*, Aug. 1, 1948, CW 19, 412). When he was on the tramp as recorded in *Down and Out in Paris and London*, he was recognized by his fellow tramps as a public school boy down on his luck. All through his life various people commented that he had an Old Etonian accent. Whatever he might have thought of public school education, he felt that his adopted son might do well by going to Westminster or Eton, where he thought of putting his name down when he was adopted. Richard Horatio Blair did go to Loretto, a leading Scottish public school, where his uncle by marriage, Avril's husband, had gone. (They raised him after Orwell's death.) And despite Orwell's lackluster record at Eton, in 2018, his son unveiled a bust of him outside the school library with a quotation from Orwell above it stating that in order to think well, one needed to write well. Whatever he might think about it, Orwell's education made important contributions to his skill as a writer. There was a considerable amount of writing combined with the alleged advantages for helping one to think and write through studying the classics.

The war ended on November 11, 1918, wildly celebrated at Eton. Even then and some years thereafter the school went through what was regarded as a rather "Bolshie" period. Some students compiled lists of those they regarded as the greatest living men, and quite a few of the boys included Lenin. They questioned the values represented by the Officer Training Corps. It no longer seemed necessary now that the war was over. Some of Orwell's contemporaries in college, calling themselves the Caucus, were active in trying to take steps towards reform. He was sympathetic to their aims but not particularly active on their behalf. Already he held the belief, so central to *Animal Farm* and *Nineteen Eighty-Four*, that changes for the better would probably not last and would be subverted by those in power. He did join with others in mocking the Officer Training Corps by singing negative new lyrics to traditional songs and wearing casual dress at the anniversary celebrations on Armistice Day, 1919.

In December 1921 he left Eton. It had continued his education as a member of the "lower-upper-middle class." Subversive as many of his thoughts and opinions might be, he had been educated at the heart of the English state. As John Strachey, an Old Etonian himself, once remarked, if there were ever a Communist government in Britain, most of the Cabinet would be Old Etonians. At a not particularly distinguished level Orwell would serve the state as an officer in the Burma police from 1922 to 1927. He and his friends might be somewhat cynical about the war. Yet being, so to speak, at a center of the English state during the war's concluding months played an important role in shaping his view of the world. Eton was the training ground for those who would be in charge. It might be understated, yet it would instill a natural assumption of authority. It even trained those who might use their skills to question and possibly change their society. Orwell had a deeply critical and perceptive mind and would become one of the most powerful and influential of English writers, best known for *Animal Farm* and *Nineteen Eighty-Four* but also for some of the most perceptive, important, and brilliant essays written in English. He might have mixed feelings about the war and questioned how much it affected his daily life while he was at St. Cyprian's and Eton. Yet the values of patriotism particularly during wartime that those schools taught were very important factors in the making of Orwell the writer and person. He never disowned what he had absorbed in his earliest years. In that central essay of 1946, "Why I Write," he evokes the importance of those days but not in political terms. "I am not able, and I do not want, completely to abandon the world-view that I acquired in childhood. So long as I remain alive and well I shall continue to feel strongly about prose style, to love the surface of the earth, and to take pleasure in solid objects and scraps of useless information" (CW 18, 319–320). After Eton he would spend five years, 1922 to 1927, serving in Burma as an officer in the Indian Imperial Police. During those years he could not be more closely identified with the Empire. The British in Burma were an occupying power and had secured the country by conquest in the nineteenth century.

War as such did not play much of a role in Orwell's life between his leaving Eton and his going to Spain. In a sense he was a member of the military as an officer in the Burmese police, living a life in Burma somewhat similar to what it might have been like if he had been an officer in the British army. He returned to England in 1927 and resigned from the police, throwing over a secure career in order to become a writer. It took him some time to achieve this aim.

He published very little before his first book, *Down and Out in Paris and London*, appeared in 1933. His first novel, *Burmese Days*, appeared in 1934. It and *Down and Out* achieved modest successes. He also started to publish in periodicals. He was becoming a writer with some reputation and some sales but not enough to support himself. He did publish two further novels, *A Clergyman's Daughter* in 1935 and *Keep the Aspidistra Flying* in 1936, both being somewhat critical accounts of aspects of English life, the latter dwelling on how much the need for money ruled it. Ultimately he wasn't very satisfied with these two books and didn't wish for them to be republished.

Just before going to Spain he finished writing *The Road to Wigan Pier*, an important, memorable, and somewhat idiosyncratic study of the effects of the Depression in England, particularly in the north. As a selection of the newly formed Left Book Club and its system of automatically sending its books, at a modest price, to its approximately 40,000 members, it became very much his best-selling book so far and made him better known. It also marked his further movement towards the left and socialism. As he wrote in the introduction to the Ukrainian edition of *Animal Farm* in 1947: "Up to 1930 I did not on the whole look upon myself as a Socialist. In fact I had as yet no clearly defined political views. I became more pro-Socialist more out of disgust with the way the poorer section of the industrial workers were oppressed and neglected than out of any theoretical admiration for a planned society" (CW 19, 87). At the same time he deplored in vivid prose, to the distress of his publisher, Victor Gollancz, what he considered the unfortunate quirks of many middle-class socialists, such as himself. He famously and unfairly caricatured them as a sandal-wearing, vegetarian, somewhat eccentric men very likely to put off members of the working class, as well as others. He also rather romanticized the working class in his depiction in *The Road to Wigan Pier* of a proletarian family at home. But at the same time, as in his famous image of a woman poking a drain and others scavenging for bits of coal, he made clear their desperate plight during the Depression. But the idea of war and its influence upon his ideas were not significant factors in his thinking in the years between the First World War and the Spanish Civil War.

The importance of the Spanish Civil War for the shaping of Orwell, unlike the significance of the First World War, has been extensively discussed by many, including myself. Indeed the central theme of William Abrahams's and my *Orwell: The Transformation* (1979) is that it was because of his experience in that war that he fully became not only the writer George Orwell but also a fully committed socialist, as he stated himself. In so many ways the six months in Spain involved with its war was the most decisive experience of his life. It released within him the energy and insight to accomplish the work by which he is best known: his two most significant and popular novels, *Animal Farm* and *Nineteen Eighty-Four,* so many of his literary and political essays, and his great book about the war itself, *Homage to Catalonia.*

He had coined the writing name George Orwell for the publication of *Down and Out in Paris and London* in 1933. Most of his publications from then on were under that name. But he was still known as Eric Blair to his friends and correspondents. After Spain, although he never legally changed his name, all his writing and much of his correspondence was in the name of George Orwell. (When it was suggested to him that he might legally change his name, he said that he would then have to find another name to write under.) Yet on his tombstone he is Eric Arthur Blair. Although he was a young cynic when he left Eton, if he were then politically on the Left it would have been unlikely that he would have become a police officer in Burma as he was from 1922 to 1927. While there and after, he increasingly became a strong anti-imperialist and leftwards leaning. In *The Road to Wigan Pier*, that investigation of the Depression that he wrote in 1936, he continued to move to the Left in his idiosyncratic way, combined with his vivid, notorious denunciation of many middle-class socialists, as he was himself.

As I stated earlier, the importance of Orwell being quite young during the First World War has not had enough attention paid to it. In those years, through family and education, much as he might question them in the future, traditional English values became and remained an important part of his makeup. There is also no question that the crucial significance of Orwell's short involvement in the Spanish Civil War from December 1936 to June 1937 was crucial in shaping his thought, writings, and actions. After his return from Burma in 1927 and his decision to resign from the police service in order to become a writer, he established himself in the following years as a known literary figure with three novels, two books of reportage, although they were in many way much more than that, and publications in periodicals. They included what would become two of his most famous and powerfully succinct essays, "Shooting an Elephant" and "A Hanging," expressing his views on Empire in vivid accounts of two of his experiences in the Indian Imperial Police. He barely made a living and had to take on some supplementary employment as a schoolteacher and later a bookstore assistant. But he did become in those years an established minor writer with an active literary agent, Leonard Moore, and a long-term relationship with Victor Gollancz, a prominent publisher.

Too young to fight, he had not been involved in the First World War. As a schoolboy he was enrolled, through no choice of his own but like every boy at his schools, first in the St. Cyprian's Cadet Corps and then in Eton's Officer Training Corps. As far as one knows, he was for most of the time too young to be cynical about the Cadet Corps. He had no choice but to fully participate in its activities. He had a much more questioning attitude about the Eton OTC after the war was over. There was no danger that he might become a young officer, a group with a high mortality rate. On the other hand, participation in the Spanish Civil War was entirely voluntary and in fact required considerable effort for him to achieve. His original thought was not go to fight, although he might have had it in his mind as possibility, but rather to write about the situation. He was completing *The Road to*

Wigan Pier when the war broke out in July 1936. Whatever his interest in it, his first priority was finishing that book. His trip to the north and his firsthand observation of the experience of the unemployed during the Depression had played an important role in moving him to the Left. It's perhaps significant that it was at this time that he wrote his most famous anti-imperialist essay, "Shooting an Elephant." The autobiographical second section of *The Road to Wigan Pier*, its most controversial part, did point out what was wrong with many middle-class socialists, such as himself, whom he cruelly satirized as sandal-wearing, off-putting, vegetarian cranks. He had much of the English gentleman's disapproving view about such individuals.

He did not go to Spain with a particular set of preconceived political ideas. Ever since his return from Burma in 1927 he had been moving to the Left, but it was not until Spain that his political ideas reached a coherent and firm shape. To be involved with the struggle against the Right in Spain was not so compelling that he had gone off to Spain when the war started. Spain would be the next project. He had married the splendid Eileen O'Shaughnessy the month before the civil war had broken out in July 1936. They were living in an austere country cottage and running a primitive small shop there. Most important, he was finishing writing *The Road to Wigan Pier* which, as an eventual selection of the Left Book Club, made him more money and had more circulation than any previous publication. (It had been commissioned by Gollancz in January 1936; the club did not come into existence until February with its first publication in May.) He was planning to deliver the manuscript in December 1936. Even the Spanish Civil War, which would have such a transformative effect upon him as a writer and as a socialist, could not distract him from his writing, although he did make some reference to the war in his text. In any case in those early days of the war he did not pay that much attention to it. At first it might have seemed to him, to the extent that he knew anything about it, a traditional Spanish conflict in which the Right was taking military steps, as it had in the past, to overthrow a more democratic government. It quite shortly, however, became an international struggle as Franco emerged as not only a military figure of the Right but as something of a Fascist, supported by Hitler and Mussolini. If France, Britain, and the United States had been willing to sell arms to the legitimate Spanish government, the Franco forces might have remained no more than an ultimately defeated native Far Right military movement, supported by the Spanish Fascist party, the Falange. In the course of the war, the Loyalists had no choice but to be dominated by Russian wishes as the Soviet Union became virtually its only supporter willing to sell it arms. The war inevitably came to have implications for the worsening international situation. What would Britain and France do? What would the Soviet Union do? Unfortunately for the Republic, Britain, France, and the United States adhered to the Non-Intervention Agreement.

Many on the Left in Britain were pacifists. Notably the Labour Party, still dominated by those who opposed war and rearmament in Britain itself, was unwilling to support coming to the aid of the Republic or making it possible for it to acquire arms from Britain.

Orwell was closely connected with the *Adelphi*, which adhered to a pacifist position. He published in it and had spoken at its summer school. Yet as time passed in the autumn of 1936, Orwell became increasingly preoccupied with Spain. He felt that he should go there himself and write about the war. Influenced one suspects by Spain in the second part of *Road to Wigan Pier* manuscript, he paid some attention to the threat of Fascism. By mid-November he had decided that he must go there at the least as a journalist. By December 11 the book was finished, typed by Eileen and ready to be sent to his publisher, Gollancz, via his agent, Leonard Moore. On December 15 he also informed Moore that he would be going to Spain. *The Road to Wigan Pier* would be published as a Left Book Club selection in March 1937, despite Gollancz's misgivings about the autobiographical second part of the book, and would be sent to its more than 40,000 members, with a preface by Gollancz pointing out his differences with his author about the defects of British socialism.

It is important to remember that Orwell was not yet an anti-Communist and had probably not thought about the Communist Party much one way or another, although of course he was aware of it. In 1932 in a letter to Eleanor

Jacques, a sometime girlfriend, he noted that "the other day I saw a man—Communist, I suppose—selling the Daily Worker, & I went up to him & said, 'Have you the D.W.?' –He: 'Yes, sir.' Dear old England!" (CW 10, 271, Oct. 19, 1932). He was rarely a joiner, and there is little sense that he had any interest in joining any political party. But he wanted to go to Spain officially as a journalist, and he felt he needed some sort of sponsorship to do so. It was in the back of his mind that he might enlist, but he was not at all sure that because of his bad health he would be accepted.

Rather wonderfully, considering his later positions, he turned first to the Communist Party. Already the party was facilitating committed young men, mostly working class, to go to Spain to fight, as others were coming from elsewhere in the world, and to join the International Brigade. It's rather nice that he used his Etonian connections to facilitate a meeting with Harry Pollitt, the General Secretary of the Party. He asked his Etonian friend, Richard Rees, to introduce him to John Strachey, an Eton contemporary of them both although Orwell hadn't known him there. Incidentally Strachey, along with Harold Laski and Gollancz—oh, how everything in England is connected in its upper reaches be they on the Left or the Right—was a selector for the Left Book Club. Strachey would know Orwell's work but would not agree with his depiction of socialism. He may not yet have read *The Road to Wigan Pier*. Strachey was not a member of the Communist Party, but he hewed at that point very closely to its line. He arranged for Orwell to meet with Pollitt, which was not a success. Pollitt was interested in writers going to Spain, and when Stephen Spender, during his brief membership in the party, asked Pollitt about that he suggested that he get himself killed in Spain and hence become the Lord Byron of the war. In their interview, Orwell expressed some sympathy for anarchism, which would have been anathema to Pollitt, and also said that if he did decide to fight he wouldn't consider joining the International Brigade until he had found out more about it once he was in Spain. Not surprisingly, Pollitt would give him no help other than mentioning that he could probably secure a safe-conduct from the Spanish embassy in Paris.

Orwell next turned to the tiny Independent Labour Party with then only about 4,000 members. In 1893 it had been one of the founding constituent members of the Labour Party itself. But it had disaffiliated from the Labour Party in 1932 and was to the left of it ideologically. If he had thought about it, Orwell might have found the party too doctrinaire for his tastes, but he doesn't appear to have worried then about such issues. This casual choice, driven by the need to find a sponsor for his trip to Spain, would have crucial consequences for the shaping of Orwell's ideas. It in effect determined what would happen to him in Spain. The Independent Labour Party (ILP) was perhaps a somewhat appropriately quirky organization for Orwell to join. Yet he needed, he felt, some official connection. The party was willing to accredit him as a correspondent for its publication, the *New Leader*. A prominent member of the party, H. N. Brailsford, a former editor of the *New Leader*, gave him a letter of introduction to John McNair, the ILP's man in Barcelona, as did Fenner Brockway, the party's General Secretary. Orwell did not join the party at this point and only did so briefly in 1938 after his return from Spain. Brailsford himself, although over sixty, wanted to go to Spain himself to fight with the International Brigade but was turned down because of his age and probably also for his anti-Stalinist views. Perhaps he wanted Orwell to fight as his replacement. And at that point Brailsford thought that British recruits should join the International Brigade. Ironically he ultimately disagreed with Orwell, perhaps surprisingly, as a member of the ILP supporting the Communist position in Barcelona during the May days the following spring.

Orwell went first to Paris to secure his safe conduct from the Spanish embassy. While there he visited Henry Miller whose writing he so admired. They had a very congenial meeting, although the apolitical Miller told him he was a fool to go to Spain but did give him a corduroy jacket to help him keep warm. The Barcelona he arrived in on December 26, 1936, was less egalitarian than it had been some months before, but it still had become a strikingly noncapitalist world after the outbreak of the civil war. Orwell found it deeply exhilarating and inspiring. He thought it was a socialist paradise. Hats and ties had vanished. Rents had been reduced by half, tipping had been abolished, 70 percent of all industry had been collectivized. It was during his time in Spain that his concept of a possible democratic socialism would take its mature form. He wasn't yet aware that this egalitarianism had already begun to decline and would so dramatically in the months to come. That trajectory as well would be crucial in shaping his ideas about how socialism could be so easily betrayed and undermined. But at this moment, whatever hesitations he had about fighting for this new society evaporated. He now wished to join a military group. He went to see John McNair to whom he had a letter of introduction, not in his capacity as a correspondent but as a potential soldier, although he might also write about the situation. McNair was at first was put off by Orwell's Etonian accent and manner, but when he discovered that Blair was Orwell, whose writings he admired, he was helpful. He checked that he wasn't a Stalinist and said he could join either the military of the Confederación Nacional del Trabajo (CNT, National Confederation of Labor), the large anarchist-inclined political group at the time dominant in Barcelona, or the Partido Obrero de Unificación Marxista (POUM, Workers' Party of Marxist Unification), the far smaller party affiliated with the Independent Labour Party. He then promptly joined the POUM militia. He went off to the Lenin barracks for a week of pretty much no training, although he, based on his school and police experience, did organize some drilling. It was there that he had by chance his handshake with an Italian militiaman who was in the group. They had no common language, but nevertheless that handshake gave him an increased sense that this was a new world well worth fighting for. As he wrote about him some years later in 1942: "In spite of power politics and journalistic lying, the central issue of the war was the attempt of people like this to win the decent life which they knew to be their birthright." The encounter produced probably Orwell's best known poetic lines: "But the thing I saw in your face/No power can disinherit:/No bomb that ever burst/Shatters the crystal spirit" (CW 13, 509–511). He had now committed himself to the military struggle against Fascism.

A week later he went to the Aragon front. He would be there for 115 days, seeing comparatively little action. There was a lot of time for talk, particularly as he was transferred to a largely English-speaking unit. Harry Milton, an American attached to the group, found Orwell politically naïve and tried to make him more familiar with the political situation, particularly the growing antagonism between the Communists and the Anarchists as well as with the POUM. The group was varied in terms of class, and in it Orwell achieved the sense of companionship that had eluded him earlier in his life. This was the sort of life that socialism could bring about. He enjoyed his comrades although some found him a bit aloof. He was clearly the English gentleman, reading Shakespeare and Charles Reade, and drinking the English tea that Eileen had procured for him from the fashionable English store Fortnum & Mason or the Army and Navy Stores in London. He was able to indulge his love of the countryside, noting the few positive signs of nature. There were some patrols and some shooting as the enemy lines were quite close. Perhaps the best known incident at this point, attesting to his fundamental humanity in a rather odd way, was his refraining from shooting at a rebel solider running along holding up his trousers. Orwell experienced in mid-April one of the few actual experiences of fighting he had at the front. The description of the event in the *New Leader* might well have been an account of an engagement in the First World War. "'Charge,' shouted Blair. . . . In front of the parapet was Eric Blair's tall figure, coolly strolling forward through the storm of fire. He leapt at the parapet, then stumbled. Hell, had they got him? No, he was over" (*New Leader,* April 30, 1937).

As he became more politically sophisticated he found himself disagreeing more and more with the POUM line which he construed as making more important the winning of the revolution than the winning of the war. By April he became increasingly committed to the idea of leaving the POUM militia and joining the International Brigade. He wanted to participate in the defense of Madrid in contrast to the comparative lack of action on the Aragon front. He also believed, rightly, that the International Brigade was much better organized than the POUM militia. Yet his views were about to dramatically change.

He returned to Barcelona in late April on leave and in order to go forward with the idea of transferring to the International Brigade. The POUM had been in ideological trouble since December as being too committed to changing society. Its leader, Andrés Nin, had been forced out of the Catalan government. It was increasingly anti-Stalinist as Russian influence was becoming more and more powerful in Spain. The Soviet Union was the only major power aiding the Republic with arms, but in return it was demanding more and more control of the Spanish state as well as payment in Spanish gold. He found a very different Barcelona from what he had experienced just four months before. A fair amount of the exhilarating egalitarianism he had so exalted earlier had disappeared. The tensions between the anarchists and the socialists, supported by the Communists, were becoming more and more palpable. Yet Orwell continued in his attempt to join the International Brigade. He might still be more in sympathy with the views of the anarchists, with whom the POUM was allied, but more important to him was a desire to be where the action was, Madrid, and to be able to play a more active role. Walter Tapsell, an English Communist charged with the task of getting English POUMists to defect, was able to arrange for him to go to Albacete, where the Brigade had its headquarters so that he could join it. He would do that after finishing his two-week leave and recovering his health. He was also waiting for a pair of boots to be made for his very large feet.

But on May 3 the situation changed dramatically. The socialists tried to take over the Telephone Exchange building from the anarchists. Fighting broke out in Barcelona between the socialists and the anarchists, supported by the POUM. Whatever his doubts about the POUM, when he saw his comrades being attacked, there was no question which side he would support. There was no way he would now join the International Brigade. He spent three nights on sentry duty on the top of the Poliorama Cinema guarding the POUM headquarters located across the street on the Ramblas. (Years ago I climbed to this roof and had a good sense of the important strategic significance of this location.) Ideology took second place to human beings, to decency. In his view, the socialists were now betraying the revolution and were increasingly returning Barcelona in particular and Spain as well to being a bourgeois democracy without the exhilaration of the egalitarian society he had found when he had first arrived. His experience in the war was absolutely crucial in forming both the positive and negative ideas that shaped his two best known novels, *Animal Farm* and *Nineteen Eighty-Four*. A socialist society was the best of all possible worlds, but it was so very difficult for it to preserve itself as those who helped create it would then become determined to hold onto their power. They would betray the revolution in the order to remain in power. POUM lost the battle in Barcelona against the main parties of the socialists, the Unified Socialist Party of Catalonia and the CNT, supported by the Communists.

POUM, as the weakest political party, was vilified as the main cause for the dissension. Orwell had abandoned any intention he might have had for joining the International Brigade. So after his leave, he returned to the front as a second lieutenant in command of a unit of thirty. And it was there on May 20 that a sniper's bullet caught

him in the throat, almost, as he thought correctly, killing
him as it just missed his carotid artery. Being so tall, he
was particularly at risk when he looked over the parapet.
By the end of May, back in Barcelona, he was on the road
to recovery although he didn't have his voice back yet. He
was of no further use as a soldier, so the intention was to
leave as soon as he was able. And now he was fed up with
the political situation, how it had betrayed what he had
construed as the ideal society of Barcelona just a few
months before. Regulations demanded that he return to
the front to secure his discharge which he was determined
to do. He was back in Barcelona on June 20, but by now
the POUM had been suppressed. By day he and Eileen
acted as tourists, by night he slept in ruined churches or
on park benches. Sometime before, Eileen had come to
Barcelona to act at John McNair's assistant, and she had
also visited Orwell at the front. In the meantime his com-
mander in the militia, Georges Kopp, had been arrested.
Orwell with extraordinary bravado and at the risk that he
might be arrested himself went to see him twice in prison
in hope that he could help secure his release. He also went
to the War Ministry on Kopp's behalf in a failed attempt
to arrange that a letter that might facilitate Kopp's release
be forwarded, even though he was told it would be. He
might have been arrested himself at both places. Perhaps
he thought that the carapace of being an English gentleman would protect him, as perhaps it did. Would those
foreigners dare to touch him? They did not. He was now
becoming fiercely anti-Communist, in good part as he

was deeply upset at the death while in captivity of a fellow British soldier in the POUM, Bob Smillie. He was the grandson of Robert Smillie, one of the founders and heroes of the Independent Labour Party. It was unclear whether Smillie had been executed or had died from medical neglect and possible abuse after being diagnosed with appendicitis. Spain was also crucial in making Orwell deeply aware of the ability of the press to report stories that were totally untrue. "Facts" could be altered to fit a political agenda. As he wrote very shortly after returning from Spain: "The Spanish war has probably produced a richer crop of lies than any event since the Great War of 1914–18" (CW ii, 41). In all these experiences one can easily see the genesis of his two most famous works.

Two days later on June 23 he and Eileen as well as John McNair and a young English fellow POUM recruit, Stafford Cottman, safely left Spain. In Spain they had been honorable members of the proletariat. Now they were acting as bourgeois as possible as that would protect them from being detained by police and border authorities, although they were searched. A warrant had been issued for their arrest, but fortunately their names were not on any lists held by those who questioned them on their way out of Spain. Orwell had lost his political innocence but oddly perhaps at the same time had firmly acquired his own brand of political idealism, a vision of a democratic socialist society might actually come about, although its survival would always be difficult. As he had written to Cyril Connolly while in the hospital recovering from his wound: "I have seen wonderful things & at last really believe in Socialism, which I never did before. On the whole, though I am sorry not to have seen Madrid, I am glad to have been on a comparatively little-known front among Anarchists & Poum people instead of in the International Brigade, as I should have been if I had come with C.P. credentials instead of I.L.P. ones" (CW 11, 28, June 8, 1937). As he wrote even more powerfully in his classic self-defining essay of 1946, "Why I Write": "Every line of serious work that I have written since 1936 has been written, directly or indirectly, *against* totalitarianism and *for* democratic Socialism, as I understand it. . . . What I have most wanted to do throughout the past ten years is to make political writing into an art. . . . Good prose is like a window-pane. . . . Looking back through my work, I see that it is invariably where I lacked a *political* purpose that I wrote lifeless books and was betrayed into purple passages, sentences without meaning, decorative adjectives and humbug generally" (CW 18, 319–320).

Despite so much despicable behavior by so many, the war experience in Spain left him with a greater faith in the fundamental decency of human beings. And with the hope that there might be someday a true socialist society, despite the great difficulties in bringing it about and the even greater problem of maintaining its existence. The Spanish Civil War was for him the most important war for the shaping of his ideas and making him an even more powerful writer. Indeed one might say it was what made him into a great writer.

For the next few years Orwell's views on war took an abrupt change. I have argued how profoundly the Spanish Civil War affected him, but it also disillusioned him. For the next two years he went through a somewhat intense and perhaps unexpected pacifist phase, a rather pragmatic antiwar set of beliefs. He did not reject the use of violence if it were to overthrow capitalism. At this point he regarded Britain and Germany and possibly the Soviet Union as imperialist powers fighting for markets with not that much to choose between them. Socialism he felt was the only real alternative to Fascism. As he wrote in a letter in August 1937: "Fascism has no real opposite except Socialism. You can't fight against Fascism in the name of 'democracy' because what we call democracy in a capitalist country only remains in being when things are going well; in time of difficulty it turns immediately into Fascism" (CW 11, 76). In a sense he now entered the most radical phase in his belief that the only way to prevent Fascism was to overthrow capitalism. These were ideas which would be further developed in the early years of the Second World War. As he wrote to Geoffrey Gorer in September 1937: "I do not see how one can oppose Fascism except for working for the overthrow of capitalism, starting, of course, in one's own country" (CW 11, 80). But on his return from Spain until the outbreak of the Second World War he came to see pacifism, since it avoided war, as what would prevent Britain from taking a Fascist turn.

He was in England until September 1938, completing *Homage to Catalonia*. During that time he had a tubercular attack which put him in a sanatorium for nearly six months. Then he and Eileen went to Morocco to regain his health, thanks to the generosity of an admirer of his work, a wealthy Old Etonian novelist, L. H. Myers, quite a few years his senior, who anonymously provided the funds. There he worked on his last 1930s novel, *Coming Up for Air*. He much preferred it to his two previous ones, *A Clergyman's Daughter* and *Keep the Aspidistra Flying*. It is infused with a love of the English countryside and an intense sense of how it was at its best before the First World War, although he approaches his central character George Bowling's nostalgia with a certain degree of irony. It also suggested the paradox of Orwell's thought and how he combined his intense love of his country as it had been before the First World War with his eventual belief of the need for it to be fundamentally changed in socialist ways. He was an extraordinary combination of a certain degree of sentimentality and hard-headedness. It fit so well with the central English paradox that explains so much about the country: its ability to dramatically change so much in order to achieve its aim to stay the same as much as possible. Similar feelings of the changes coming that would so challenge traditional England can be found in the well-known last lines of *Homage to Catalonia*, which record his thoughts about southern England while on the train back to London on his return from Spain.

> Down here it was still the England I had known in my childhood: the railway-cuttings smothered in wild flowers, the deep meadows where the great shining horses browse and meditate, the slow-moving streams bordered by willows, the green bosoms of the elms, the larkspurs in the cottage gardens; and then the huge peaceful wilderness of outer London, the barges on the miry river, the familiar streets, the posters telling of cricket matches and Royal weddings, the men in bowler hats, the pigeons in Trafalgar Square, the red buses, the blue policemen—all sleeping the deep, deep sleep of England, from which I sometimes fear that we shall never wake till we are jerked out of it by the roar of bombs.

Although Spain had solidified his commitment to democratic socialism, it also left him bitterly disillusioned about the Spanish government, now so beholden for support to the Russians. At this point he thought waging war was not the solution, and hence Britain should refuse to do so. Britain going to war, he felt, would provide the excuse for a Fascist regime to be imposed in Britain itself. That September he signed a manifesto with 148 others in the Independent Labour Party (ILP) publication, the *New Leader*, taking a strong position against war. "We repudiate, therefore, all appeals to the people to support a war which would, in fact, maintain and extend imperialist possessions and interests. . . . If war comes, it will be our duty to resist, and to organise such opposition that will hasten the end of that war, not by Treaties which represent the triumph of one imperialism over another, and which would only sow the seeds of future wars, but by the building of a new world order based on fellowship and justice" (CW 11, 213). The previous June, declaring himself an active socialist, he supported the ILP by joining the party, but he didn't remain a member for long. He felt, quite unrealistically, that there could be a popular antiwar movements not only in Britain and France but also in the Germany and Italy. In a letter to Herbert Read in January, 1939, he wrote that those opposed to war would need to consider organizing illegal activity to do so, but it seems that he had nothing further in mind than underground publications. He wrote to Richard Rees's mother in February, "The idea of war is just a nightmare to me, and I refuse to believe that it can do the slightest good or even that it makes much difference who wins" (CW 11, 330). In a letter to Geoffrey Gorer in January 1939 he remarked that "when I hear people tirading against Hitler nowadays I often think the clock has somehow slipped back twenty years" as if Hitler weren't very different from the Kaiser

THE SECOND WORLD WAR

(CW 11, 321). He was certainly at this point very much against going to war against Germany. In a review as late as June 1939 he wrote that "events since 1935 had made it perfectly clear that most (but not quite all) of what now goes by the name of 'antifascism' is simply a thin disguise for jingo imperialism" (CW 11, 354).

In August 1939 he reversed his position entirely, triggered by the signing of the Russo-German pact that month. The night before the news came that Ribbentrop, the German Foreign Minister, had flown to Moscow, he had a dream that war had been declared and that he would now support it enthusiastically. As he remarked in his wonderfully entitled essay "My Country Right or Left" about the dream: "It taught me two things, first, that I should be simply relieved when the long-dreaded war started, secondly, that I was patriotic at heart. . . . What I knew in my dream that night was that the long drilling in patriotism which the middle classes go through had done its work, and that once England was in a serious jam it would be impossible for me to sabotage" (CW 12, 271). He had been very much against going to war. Now he felt quite the contrary, and he wrote very negatively about the pacifists whom he had been supporting, that they were, in effect, objectively, supporting the Nazis. He did gently apologize for this position in one of his "As I Please" columns for *Tribune* in December 1944: "I have been guilty of saying this myself more than once" (CW 16, 495). Now that the two powers he regarded so negatively had joined together he no longer felt that a war against Germany would be a serious mistake. Unusually, he combined the growing intensity of his patriotism with another powerful conviction. In order to preserve England a revolution would be necessary. "Only revolution can save England, that has been obvious for years, but now [writing in 1940] the revolution has started, and it may proceed quite quickly if only we can keep Hitler out. . . . I dare say the London gutters will have to run with blood. All right, let them if it is necessary. But when the red militias are billeted in the Ritz I shall still feel that the England I was taught to love so long ago and for such different reasons is somehow persisting" (CW 12, 271–272). Although he had rejected it before, perhaps he was now influenced by the POUM line that the war and the social revolution were inseparable.

On September 3, 1939, Britain went to war with Germany. With the outbreak of war his patriotism that had taken shape before and during the First World War and the democratic socialism that he had committed to because of his experience in the Spanish Civil War merged. He was now even more a committed patriotic socialist. Within days he had put his name down on the Central Registry indicating his desire to help in the war effort. He was now in the process of dramatically reversing his earlier position. For two years he had seen war as the enemy of socialism. Now he was coming to believe that the demands of war would facilitate, indeed require, the establishment of a socialist state. He wanted to help bring that about through being as active as he could be in supporting the war effort. As he wrote to Geoffrey Gorer on January 10, 1940, "It seems to me that now we are in this bloody war we have got to win it & I would like to lend a hand" (CW 12, 6). He did not quite lose his somewhat paradoxical attitude towards the war. He wrote a review of *Mein Kampf* for the *New English Weekly* on March 15, 1940, in which he made some rather surprising, almost shocking, remarks about Hitler. "I should like to put it on record that I've never been able to dislike Hitler. Ever since he came to power—till then, like nearly everyone, I had been deceived into thinking that he did not matter—I have reflected that I would certainly kill him if I could get within reach of him, but that I could feel no personal animosity. The fact is that there is something deeply appealing about him" (CW 12, 117).

As an example of how frequently Orwell changed or indeed reversed his views, he became strongly anti-pacifist, contrary to the position he had held firmly for two years. To be a pacifist meant he thought that objectively one was pro-Fascist as it would pave the way for a Fascist government to take over Britain. He tried to join some regular military units but was turned down on medical grounds. With his age and bad health the most he could achieve was becoming a member of the Home Guard, a part-time commitment. He thought rather unrealistically it had the potential of becoming a People's Army and that it might even be the force to bring about a revolution in Britain itself. On June 22, 1940, he published a letter in *Time and Tide* stating that an inevitable German invasion was imminent and to counter it the people needed to be armed. Then, presumably shortly after writing the letter, he wrote in his diary, "I think we have all been rather hasty in assuming that Hitler will now invade England, indeed it has been so generally expected that one might almost infer from this that he wouldn't do it." But he then went on to say, "If the invasion happens and fails, all is well, and we shall have a definitely leftwing government and a conscious movement against the governing class" (CW 12, 195–196).

When the Blitz started in September 1940, it was almost as if he were in Barcelona again. He had moved from Wallington in order to be more of a participant in this patriotic war. He had a similar sense of changes that were coming about in society, although, as in Spain, even when it was still a republic, the transformation was ultimately far less than he wished. He was welcomed in the Home Guard because of his Spanish experience and was made a sergeant in charge of ten men. His schoolboy training as well might have been relevant. He was rather dubious about the skills of the rather Colonel Blimp–like figures who had been officers in the First World War and now became officers in the Home Guard. In order to prepare the soldiers he commanded, he gave talks to his group about techniques of street fighting. A major trainer of Home Guard soldiers was Tom Wintringham who had held a major post in the International Brigade. Orwell worked with him at the Home Guard training center established at Osterley Park, the Robert Adam country house in west London. He was very anxious to participate in a military way in defending his country. He felt that his Spanish experience would be valuable particularly if Britain were invaded and hence there might be guerilla warfare. He did harbor some hopes that the Home Guard, probably not too realistically, would turn into a socialist force. This would be one way that war might help to bring about socialism. As he wrote in *Tribune* in December 1940, "For the first time in British history the chance exists for Socialists to have a certain amount of influence in the armed forces of the country" (CW 12, 310).

As he was trying at this point to play a more active political role, he felt he didn't have the concentration necessary to write a novel. So he turned his attention to shorter pieces, somewhat out of his line movie and play reviews for *Time and Tide*, the liberal feminist journal. He managed in 1940 to review more than a one hundred books as well as to write some of his most important longer essays for *Horizon* edited by his friend Cyril Connolly. *Horizon* was one of Connolly's major achievements, keeping culture alive during wartime and incidentally providing a venue for Orwell to write at length. The pieces reflected his growing interest in the nature of his own society, which he could write brilliantly and incisively about. In such essays as "Boys' Weeklies" and "The Art of Donald McGill" he became a pioneer, to a considerable degree a founder, of the serious investigation of popular culture. These were profoundly innovative and ultimately very influential works. During the war, he also wrote a series of illuminating and informative "London Letters" for the left-wing but anti-Communist American publication *Partisan Review*. In a passing remark there was a foreshadowing in the "Letters," but from the opposite political perspective, of the list he made shortly before his death of those he believed to be Communist sympathizers. He was discussing those such as Ezra Pound who had become a vehement supporter of Fascism. "If the Germans got to England, similar things would happen, and I think I could make out at least a preliminary list of the people who would go over"(CW 13, 113, Jan. 1, 1942).

It is striking that he should publish during the Second World War in 1940 his short essay "My Country Right or Left." There he discussed, as I've mentioned before, how patriotism was instilled in him while he was very young before the First World War. Now, much older, he was having similar feelings. But his ideas had been much changed by his commitment to socialism. He might be called a revolutionary patriot.

His most important publication during the war was *The Lion and the Unicorn.* He had established cordial relations with Fredric Warburg, the publisher of *Homage to Catalonia*, who was his corporal in his Home Guard unit. Through Warburg he met Tosco Fyvel. Somewhat improbably he would become a very good friend, although Orwell was unsympathetic to his passionate Zionism. Fyvel's parents, active and distinguished Zionists, had come to England before Hitler but then moved to Palestine. It

was Fyvel's original idea that something should be written about war aims. Warburg had published his book,
No Ease in Zion, and Fyvel brought his publishing idea
to him. Orwell, Fyvel, Warburg, and the German refugee, Sebastian Haffner, met in Warburg's London flat as
well as in the garden of his country cottage in Twyford,
Berkshire, to discuss this possibility while the Battle of
Britain took place over their heads. (It's a nice touch that
considering Orwell's rather ambivalent attitude towards
Jews that Fyvel and Warburg were Jewish and that Haffner, though not Jewish, was a refugee from Germany.)
They decided to launch a series of very short books or
perhaps more accurately long pamphlets, Searchlight
Books, to be edited by Fyvel and Orwell. The tracts were
to discuss desirable changes in Britain that should come
about while the country was at war to make it a country
more worth fighting for as well as to help the war effort.
And eventually they ventured into other areas. It was
announced rather grandly that "it is the aim of SEARCH-
LIGHT BOOKS to do all in their power to criticise and
kill what is rotten in Western civilisation and supply con-
structive ideas for the difficult period ahead of us. The
series . . . will stress Britain's international and imperial
responsibilities and the aim of a planned Britain at the
head of a greater and freer British Commonwealth"
(quoted in Bernard Crick, *George Orwell,* Boston: Atlan-
tic Monthly Press, 1980, 273). Orwell and Fyvel were
deeply involved with the series during most of its brief
existence. It flourished in 1941 as Orwell could devote

more time to it before being employed by the BBC. It was later curtailed by Warburg's press experiencing a shortage of paper, largely caused by the Blitz hitting its supplies. It was rather dramatic that the future of Britain was being discussed during the worst days of the London Blitz. The books began very successfully with Orwell's own work, *The Lion and the Unicorn*, the first published in the series. He was becoming better known as indicated by Penguin reissuing his *Down and Out in Paris and London* in an edition of 55,000 in December 1940.

The short Searchlight Books were priced at a modest two shillings. Originally the price was to be only a shilling, but Orwell's text was too long to be published at that price. Ultimately ten titles appeared. Among the most interesting was Ritchie Calder's *The Lesson of London* where he pointed out that the experience of the Blitz in London made it evident how essential and necessary it was for the government to take a much more active role in the welfare of all its citizens. T. C. Worsley in *The End of the Old School Tie* argued that the public schools would have to be much reformed and incorporated into a truly public system in the postwar world—slightly ironic as he had gone to Marlborough himself where he was a star cricketer. As Orwell wrote in its foreword: "The Searchlight Books have been planned to deal with the immediate rather than the distant future. Certain problems, however, are bound to arise in an urgent form as soon as the war is over and are likely to be dealt with in some shoddy makeshift way unless they are thought out in detail beforehand" (CW 12, 486). The most successful in the series was *The English at War* by Cassandra, the pen name of William Connor, the very popular columnist in the *Daily Mirror*. In it, he very briefly told amusing stories about how the English were coping and railed against the powers that be. It sold more than 30,000 copies. Orwell's *The Lion and the Unicorn* was the next best seller at approximately 12,500 copies. The books were not exclusively domestic. Arturo Barea wrote *Struggle for the Spanish Soul* about the Spanish Civil War in which he had played an active role on the Republic's side. Orwell admired his first volume of autobiography, *The Forge,* reviewing it both in *Time and Tide* and *Horizon*. Its editor, Orwell's old friend, Cyril Connolly, was scheduled to write for the series *Artist and the New World* but characteristically never did so. Sebastian Haffner one of the original planners of the series wrote *Offensive against Germany* dealing with how to wage the propaganda war. Orwell admired the novels by Joyce Cary and commissioned him to write about the future of Britain in Africa, *The Case for African Freedom*. The last text to be published, in 1942, was *Life and the Poet* by Stephen Spender. It officially was number eighteen, but eight titles that had been announced never appeared, including one by Arthur Koestler and another by G. E. Catlin, Vera Brittain's husband, about whether Britain and the United States should unite.

I would like to look at *The Lion and the Unicorn* with its somewhat contradictory subtitle, *Socialism and the*

English Genius, in a little more detail. It is a very important Orwell text in marking his commitment to democratic socialism. Published in February 1941 at the height of the Blitz, it makes very clear how important the advent of the war was in shaping Orwell's ideas. He committed himself in this work even more deeply to being an intense patriot and socialist. As he wrote in *Tribune* in darker and larger type on December 20, 1940, "We are in a strange period of history in which a revolutionary has to be a patriot and a patriot has to be a revolutionary" (CW 12, 311). He was rather sweeping in his views. He wrote in *The Left News* in January 1941, "We cannot beat Hitler without passing through revolution, nor consolidate our revolution without beating Hitler. . . . A victory over Hitler demands the destruction of capitalism. . . . Either we turn this war into a revolutionary war or we lose it" (CW 12, 346–349).

The lion and the unicorn are the heraldic beasts that support the royal coat of arms. The text both celebrates a very traditional England with its many rather sweeping generalizations about its nature as found in various aspects, in his view generally gentle, of English life. At the same time it marked more vividly than he had ever written before his admiration and commitment to the English working class, which would play a major role in his belief that the hope for salvation in *Nineteen Eighty-Four* might be found in the proles. He tended to romanticize, perhaps legitimately, what he saw as their virtues, their dislike of pretension, their lifestyle, their empiricism, their belief in the fairness of the law, and, to his mind that supreme virtue, their commitment to human decency. These might well be factors that could humanize socialism. He did not neglect the middle class and hoped that it might finally produce a new sort of intelligentsia, not the more theoretical sort that could lead to totalitarian thinking but in the English empirical tradition that could help achieve a democratic socialist society. These hopes are combined with powerful assertions of the imperative need for radical changes, which, as suggested by the subtitle, the "English genius" will make possible so as to keep the positive aspects of English life.

Yet he recognized the ability of English institutions to preserve so much of themselves, to change radically yet, paradoxically, manage to look much the same. As he began the review of a book about Eton in 1948, "It is hard to disentangle admiration from dismay when one learns that Eton in 1948 is almost exactly what it was in 1918" (CW 19, 412). It is, I believe, in the long tradition of how some reform often takes place and is thought about in England. I've often cited elsewhere the peroration of Thomas Babington Macaulay's speech in Parliament in March 1831 in support of the much debated and controversial Great Reform Act, passed in 1832. It was such a significant step in moving England slowly, though in so many ways forward, towards becoming a more democratic society. The act expanded the franchise to include the male middle class, establishing, perhaps reluctantly but claiming otherwise, that the franchise might be further broadened, as it was in the following years. Macaulay's phrase might be taken for representing much of what Orwell believed about his beloved England: "Reform so you may preserve." As Macaulay went on hyperbolically to conclude: "Renew the youth of the State. Save the multitude, endangered by its own ungovernable passions. Save the aristocracy, endangered by its own unpopular power. Save the greatest, and the fairest and most highly civilised community that ever existed."

In *The Lion and the Unicorn* Orwell made explicit the connection between what he had experienced during the First World War and what he was feeling at the time of the Second. His attitude earlier towards the First World War was mostly dismissive, but yet it had added to some extent to the foundation of patriotism he had acquired before the war itself. Orwell's take on the Second World War dramatically revived and strengthened his patriotism. As he wrote in "My Country Right or Left" a few months before in 1940, "You felt yourself a little less of a man because you had missed it [the war]. . . . Patriotism has nothing to do with conservatism. It is devotion to something that is changing but is felt to be mystically the same. (CW 12, 270–271). Orwell's view of patriotism, its influence upon him, and its relevance for the Second World War were vastly expanded in this short book of sixty-four pages. He felt very strongly that the war presented both the opportunity and the necessity for radical change while keeping loyal to the basic and ancient values of his country. He wrote a series of wonderful generalizations about the many subdued virtues of the English, particularly to be found he thought in the working class. He emphasized their dislike of war and the military. While he was writing it, Eileen wrote to a close friend in December 1940 that the book was "explaining how to be a Socialist though Tory" (Peter Davison, ed., *The Lost Orwell,* London: Timewell Press, 2006, 80). This was an amused exaggeration, but it does suggest how he might legitimately be viewed. It is rather similar to his sister Avril calling him a Tory Anarchist, a term Orwell himself applied to Swift.

Because of the necessity to win the war, Orwell felt that profound changes were necessary. On April 11, 1940, he had written Humphry House, "I think it is vitally necessary to do something towards equalising incomes, abolishing class privilege [*sic*] and setting free the subject peoples. Not to put it on any wider ground, I don't believe the war can otherwise be won" (CW 12, 140). Orwell predicted, inaccurately, that rather extreme measures might well be necessary during the war to bring about this new more egalitarian society, necessary if the war was to be won. It was undoubtedly true that the state did become much more powerful in its organizing for war purposes but not necessarily in socialist directions. Orwell believed that socialism was necessary immediately if Britain was to win the war: state ownership of the means of production and the elimination of all class privileges. He felt that the upper classes were misbehaving and asserting themselves despite there being a war on, that there were deep inequalities. "It is only by revolution that the native genius of the English people can be set free. . . . Whether it happens with or without bloodshed is largely an accident of time and place. . . . Patriotism, against which the Socialists fought so long, has become a tremendous lever in their hands" (CW 12, 415–421). The war led him to believe in the absolute necessity of the establishment of socialism in England. He turned out to be wrong.

England did establish a war economy. There was a growing but far from total equality of sacrifice from all classes. But the much more radical transformation that Orwell called for turned out not to be necessary in order eventually to win the war, particularly after the Soviet Union and the United States had entered it. Although *The Lion and the Unicorn* is full of Orwell's disdain both for the intelligentsia of the Left and for a Labour Party in his view too committed to trade union interests, under the impact of the war there was a significant shift in his thinking in an ever more radical socialist direction. One might say his analysis was to a degree correct but not in a way he anticipated. What he felt needed to happen did not take place during the war itself. Yet the Beveridge Report of 1942 promised and ultimately later delivered not a socialist society but a welfare state, perhaps, in the English way, something of a halfway house. After the war there was a considerable degree of nationalization of the means of production as well as the National Health Service and other changes in society. But it was without the power grab by the leaders of the change which Orwell had seen as the destroyer of a good society in Spain and at Animal Farm and in Oceania.

The first section of *The Lion and the Unicorn* is "England Your England," which had been published separately earlier in *Horizon* in December 1940. It begins: "As I write, highly civilized human beings are flying overhead, trying to kill me" (CW 12, 392). Orwell does not feel any animosity towards them. They are doing their duty, in his view, as patriotic Germans. He regards the power of patriotism as stronger than Christianity or socialism. And turning to England, he argues that it is different from any other country; he believes firmly in national differences. He provides a list of English characteristics and their continuity over the years: lorries, clogs, old maids, queues, gloomy Sundays, red-pillar boxes, love of flowers. England's future will be determined by what it was in the past. He does believe in some of the standard clichés about the English that might be quite unfair or at least exaggerations: they are not artistic, musical, or intellectual. He does soundly support the received position of English life, whether actually correct or not, that it is profoundly gentle and possesses a hatred of war and militarism. Many who lived in the British Empire might not agree with that assessment. But in Orwell's view, the English working class hardly knows that the Empire exists and doesn't care very much about it. It is true that other countries might not celebrate what were in fact defeats, ranging from the events of Tennyson's poem "The Charge of the Light Brigade" many years earlier to the massive military disaster but also somehow triumph of the Dunkirk evacuation that had taken place some months before Orwell was writing. As he points out, the most remembered battles of the First World War were notorious for how many British died in them and were frequently associated with strategic mistakes. He also believes that the English have great respect for the law, even if they believe it might be excessively severe. He reasserts that the English are profoundly patriotic, with an underside of being anti-foreign. Despite the lack of artistic talent in many fields, the English do excel in the one art that cannot cross borders in its original form: literature. And in these pages there emerged his famous definition of England:

> England is the most class-ridden country under the sun. . . . But in any calculation about it one has got to take into account its emotional unity, the tendency of nearly all its inhabitants to feel alike and act together in moments of supreme crisis. . . . England is not the jeweled isle of Shakespeare's much-quoted passage, nor is it the inferno depicted by Dr. Goebbels. More than either it resembles a family, a rather stuffy Victorian family, with not many black sheep in it but with all its cupboards bursting with skeletons. It has rich relations who have to be kow-towed to and poor relations who are horribly sat upon, and there is a deep conspiracy of silence upon the source of the family income. It is a family in which the young are generally thwarted and most of the power is in the hands of irresponsible uncles and bedridden aunts. Still, it is a family. It has its private language and its common memories, and at the approach of an

enemy it closes its ranks. A family with the wrong members in control—that, perhaps, is as near as one can come to describing England in a phrase. (CW 12, 400–401)

In many ways, Orwell is in a strong English tradition of radicalism, going back to the Chartists in the first half of the nineteenth century or even earlier. This tradition is represented by a strong belief in the "common people," the working class and their innate decency, virtues that Orwell held in high esteem and which he contrasted, to their disadvantage, to the values held, radical as they might be, by middle-class intellectuals. He fit easily into and valued the English disdain for theory and its emphasis on empiricism. It was the strain in English radicalism that so distressed Marx and justified the belief, probably accurate, that English radicalism owed more to Methodism than to Marxism. So in that sense Orwell was, as demonstrated in *The Lion and the Unicorn*, very much in an English tradition of radical thought.

The members of the family he felt were doing the most harm were the Blimps likely to be in charge of the Home Guard, because of their lack of intelligence, and, at the other end of the spectrum, the intelligentsia for their lack of patriotism. "They take their cookery from Paris and their opinions from Moscow. . . . The Bloomsbury highbrow, with his mechanical snigger, is as out of date as the cavalry colonel. . . . Patriotism and intelligence will have to come together again. It is the fact that we are fighting a war, and a very peculiar kind of war, that may make this possible" (CW 12, 406–407). He felt that in the years between the wars many of the older class distinctions had been breaking down. Though there were still considerable disparities of income, more and more of the population were enjoying a middle-class style of life. The war itself he thought would eliminate most of the existing class privileges. This led to one of the most lyrical and well-known passages in the work. It contained two sets of rather contradictory predictions of what England would be like after the war. Certainly the changes that he posited did not happen, except presumably for the general use of the tractor. Yet the welfare state did take some steps in the directions he suggested. "The gentleness, the hypocrisy, the thoughtlessness, the reverence for law and the hatred for uniforms will remain, along with the suet puddings and the misty skies. . . . The Stock Exchange will be pulled down, the horse plough will give way to the tractor, the country houses will be turned into children's holiday camps, the Eton and Harrow match will be forgotten, but England will still be England, an everlasting animal stretching into the future and the past, and, like all living things, having the power to change out of recognition and yet remain the same" (CW 12, 409). It was if he were a disciple of both Thomas Paine and Edmund Burke.

In the second section, "Shopkeepers at War," Orwell continued his political and economic analysis, writing while the Blitz was going on. He felt that the war clearly demonstrated that capitalism did not work. He felt, as he had been stating for some time, that there needed to be a planned economy in order to win the war, which should include common ownership of the means of production, equality of income, and the abolition of all hereditary privilege. Capitalism in England had failed to prepare for war because, according to Orwell, there was little profit in armaments. Now vast changes were necessary.

> It is only by revolution that the native genius of the English people can be set free. Revolution does not mean red flags and street fighting, it means a fundamental shift of power. Whether it happens with or without bloodshed is largely an accident of time and place. . . . What is wanted is a conscious open revolt by ordinary people against inefficiency, class privilege and the rule of the old. . . . In the short run, equality of sacrifice. . . . It is very necessary that industry be nationalized, but it is more urgently necessary that such monstrosities as butlers and "private incomes" should disappear forthwith. (CW 12, 415)

It is striking that like a true Englishman, Orwell thought in traditional class terms.

The third section is "The English Revolution." As he wrote yet again, "The war and the revolution are inseparable" (CW 12, 418). It was almost as if he would make revolution come about by repeating this mantra. He did turn out to be wrong, although to a degree the postwar welfare state had important elements of a social revolution. During the war Orwell was both at his most revolutionary and his most patriotic. He argued here the need for a socialist party that had the mass of the people behind it. This transformation to a socialist society had to happen as soon as possible in order to win the war. But he was not specific on why it was so necessary, beyond the assertion that it was so. And it certainly did not turn out to be true that the English people needed the promise of a socialist society in order to support the war. William Beveridge's *Full Employment in a Free Society* was issued in 1942. Though very important, it was of little interest to Prime Minister Churchill, and there is little indication that because of it the working class committed itself to fighting for the state. Probably most in the working class were patriotic, and many might have been socialists, but there is no indication that, contrary to Orwell, the two were necessarily connected. And there is little evidence, also contrary to what he saw as a necessity, of pressure from the working class to take immediate steps to make the country more socialistic. But it is true, as I argued in my book *The First Day of the London Blitz*, that faced with the plight of those who were bombed out in London and elsewhere, the state increasingly recognized its obligation to help all its citizens, no matter what their status might be, whether or not they might be members of the deserving or the undeserving poor or indeed of higher class status. On the other hand, in terms of Orwell's thought, it is significant that war had convinced him of the connection between war and social action, that war was indeed the possible precipitator of important social change. He felt that the Labour Party was not yet a satisfactory vehicle for this change as its main concerns were driven by the unions. The party, he believed, had supported capitalism and the Empire as it felt they were essential for the prosperity that enabled the workers to be better paid. Now the war presented a golden and necessary opportunity for the triumph of a genuine socialism. "A Socialist movement which can swing the mass of the people behind it, drive the pro-Fascists out of positions of control, wipe out the grosser injustices and let the working class see that they have something to fight for, win over the middle classes instead of antagonizing them, produce a workable imperial policy instead of a mixture of humbug and Utopianism, bring patriotism and intelligence into partnership—for the first time, a movement of such kind becomes possible. . . . War is the greatest of all agents of change" (CW 12, 421).

He appreciated that there might well be violent opposition to the transformation of society. He believed that there needed to be a nationalization of land, banks, mines, and other major industries, and limitation of income as well as Dominion status for India. This would create a socialist democracy. He did recognize that much educational reform could not take place until after the war, although he felt that both the public schools and the universities should be filled with scholarship students chosen strictly on the basis of ability. He felt that the public schools were little more than places that supported snobbery and that most of the private elementary schools should be eliminated. He did not mention that such had been his own schooling. He did recognize that not all of what he wished could be carried out immediately, but he thought it was essential that the directions be indicated. He also felt that the present government, led by Churchill, needed to be replaced in a General Election. The House of Lords should go, but probably not the monarchy. Perhaps the title of the book indicated that he thought the monarchy might support change. The Church of England would be disestablished. What he does not discuss is how all this would come about and that it would be necessary for the state to use its power to achieve these changes. Would it? The possible subsequent love of power might well be the destructive element that might impede a socialist society coming about or destroy it, dominant themes in *Animal Farm* and *Nineteen Eighty-Four*.

He reiterated his commitment to patriotism. "Patriotism has nothing to do with Conservatism. It is actually the opposite of Conservatism, since it is a devotion to something that is always changing and yet is felt to be mystically the same. It is the bridge between the future and the past" (CW 12, 428). He recognized that patriotism was not totally an attractive concept. As he wrote sometime later in an essay on H. G. Wells published in *Horizon* in August 1941: "What has kept England on its feet during the past year? In part, no doubt, some vague idea about a better future, but chiefly the atavistic emotion of patriotism, the ingrained feeling of the English-speaking peoples that they are superior to foreigners" (CW 12, 537–538). Through revolution Orwell believed England would actually become more herself. *The Lion and the Unicorn*, its message summed up in its title and subtitle, *Socialism and the English Genius*, was a powerful polemical piece of writing. But it is not surprising that Orwell didn't want it reprinted. So much of what he hoped for, so much that he thought was necessary, didn't happen. To a degree progressive change happened but certainly far less than he wanted and predicted. There was the establishment of the welfare state after the war, most notably marked by the introduction of the National Health Service. Many industries were nationalized though eventually quite a few were returned to private ownership. To a greater degree education at the secondary and tertiary levels was increasingly based on merit. But the public schools were as strong as ever. India and Pakistan became independent nations. The Empire disintegrated. The House of Lords was not abolished, but it became dominated by life peers. The Anglican Church was not disestablished. It was not necessary, as he thought, that socialism be established as soon as possible for the war to be won.

Yet the sort of country that he envisioned did to some considerable degree come about. At the same time, it remained loyal to Macaulay's dictum that one should reform in order to preserve. I'm sure that Orwell would have a lot to complain about in contemporary England. Yet in so many ways it is a society that has both profoundly changed and yet preserves much of its past. The demands of war motivated Orwell to argue for the necessity of such changes not only for their own sake, but also because he believed they needed to happen in order to win the war. But he was never all that specific how such changes or even the promise of them would inspire greater efforts to win the war. Did the Beveridge Plan inspire the public? It might have been a minor factor but hardly a major one. Although not achieved to the degree that he might have wished, change did ultimately take place after the war, and the war was probably a necessary precondition. War played a crucial role in shaping his thinking about what changes were necessary not only to win the war but to make the country a more egalitarian and socialist society. As he wrote in *The Left News* in April 1941: "What Socialists of, I should say, nearly all schools believe is that the destiny and therefore the true happiness of man lies in a society of true communism, that is to say a society in which all human beings are more or less equal, in which no one has the power to oppress another, in which economic motives have ceased to operate, in which men are governed by love and curiosity and not by greed and fear" (CW 12, 459). On the other hand he could also be rather grim in the expectation for the future. As he wrote in his "War-time Diary" on May 18, 1941: "Within two years we shall either be conquered or we shall be a Socialist republic fighting for its life, with a secret police force and half the population starving" (CW 12, 501).

From August 1941 to November 1943 Orwell's life was dominated by his working for the BBC, having accepted a job arranging talks by others and himself, as well as broadcasting them, for the Indian section of the Eastern service. During the period he conducted a vast correspondence, much of it routine, with numerous individuals, including T. S. Eliot and E. M. Forster, about possible talks and more pedestrian matters. It is rather intriguing that he was inconsistent about what name he signed his letters, more often as Eric Blair, the name he was employed under, but also in quite a few letters George Orwell, mostly to literary figures who might be familiar with his writings. At times he used both of his names, signing himself E.A.B. George Orwell.

He had rather mixed feelings about the position and the BBC itself. In a sense he was doing his bit for the war effort, helping and hoping that the broadcasts would increase Indian commitment to the cause. Reading the texts of those broadcasts that have survived, they were impressive. They were mostly about cultural topics rather than heavy-handed propaganda efforts. Most weeks he also broadcast a straightforward news review. Most notably he organized a broadcast literary magazine, *Voice*, which included contemporary poetry generally read by its author, including such eminent figures as T. S. Eliot. He was skeptical about how many in India actually listened to the broadcasts. And as he wrote about the BBC itself in his "War-time Diary" on March 14, 1942, perhaps exaggerating somewhat: "*Its atmosphere is something half way between a girls' school and a lunatic asylum, and all we are doing at present is useless, or slightly worse than useless. . . . All propaganda is lies, even when one is telling the truth.*

I don't think this matters so long as one knows what one is doing, and why" (CW 13, 229, his italics). In his letter of resignation on September 24, 1943, he said he felt that he had been wasting his time and that the work had not produced any results, on the basis of a survey that had been taken demonstrating that few listened. Yet the many broadcasts he did create were on the whole very impressive although it could be said that they were very England-centered, which, of course, was what he knew about, although he did know about the Empire as well. They presented the culture that the English were fighting for as well as other aspects of the war but did not seem planned to particularly appeal to their intended Indian audience.

He did edit a book, *Talking to India*, published in November 1943. It consisted of a selection of twenty-two of the forty-five-minute talks given on the service. Of the pieces twelve were given by Asians, including the novelist Mulk Raj Anan who worked in the service and became of friend of Orwell's. Two were given by E. M. Forster, who had a long-standing interest in India, but neither centered on India. Only six of the talks actually had Asian themes. Rather extraordinarily the collection also included a talk by Subhas Chandra Bose from Berlin, obviously not given on the service. He had defected to the Axis and committed himself to leading troops in Asia against the British in order to free his country. In his introduction Orwell justifies the inclusion while denouncing Bose.

In Orwell's own other broadcasts—he only includes one of his own in the book—there was scant justification

given why Indians should be wholehearted supporters
of British culture. But discussing their culture was what
the British participants could do best. Many of the broadcasts in the Indian service were given and written by
Indians, and they presumably would have more Indian
references and may well have dealt more directly with
India itself. Quite a few Indians were involved both in
both the creating and broadcasting. The mixture of participants is suggested by the well-known photograph of
ten of the participants: evenly divided between Asians
and non-Asians, the latter including Orwell himself as
well as T. S. Eliot and William Empson. But when Orwell
listed names of the participants they were almost exclusively English. One justification for such a considerable
concentration on the English-speaking and on English
subjects was the assumption that a considerable number
of the listeners were or had been at Indian universities
studying English literature. Orwell himself was a firm
supporter of more and more autonomy, at least Dominion status, for India, but that was not reflected in the
broadcasts. He felt that it was a necessary step—though
it didn't prove to be during the war itself—to secure victory. There is no indication that he tried to incorporate
such ideas into the broadcasts, and it is likely that if he
had done so, such texts might have been censored out. A
good portion of the broadcasts were straightforward news
reports written by Orwell, although the cultural pro-
grams in and of themselves were very impressive. But
whatever his accomplishments may have been, he had

now come to the conclusion that he could make a more
effective and satisfactory, to him, contribution through
journalism outside of the BBC.

Despite his call for the necessity of immediate action,
Orwell continued to lament the state of English society
even under the pressure of war. As he wrote in his "London Letter" to the *Partisan Review*, composed in May
1942 and published in its July-August issue: "The basic
fact is that people are now as fed up and as ready for a
radical policy as they were at the time of Dunkirk. . . .
The war has brought the class nature of their society very
sharply home to English people. . . . There is the unmis-
takable fact that all real power depends on class privilege. . . . We can't win the war with our present social
and economic structure" (CW 13, 302–307). He predicted quite wrongly that Churchill would not remain
in power much longer and that it was likely that he
would be replaced by Stafford Cripps. In his "London
Letter" for November-December 1942 he still seemed to
feel that socialism needed to come about to win the war
but it wasn't happening. "One can predict the future in
the form of an 'either-or': either we introduce Socialism,
or we lose the war. The strange, perhaps disquieting fact
is that it was as easy to make this prophecy in 1940 as it
is now, and yet the essential situation has barely altered.
We have been two years on the burning deck and somehow the magazine never explodes" (CW 13, 522). But
then in the "London Letter" of March-April 1943, writ-

ten in January, he appears to have given up hope that anything approaching a revolution might happen.

> The forces of reaction have won hands down. Churchill is firm in the saddle again, Cripps has flung away his chances, no other leftwing leader or movement has appeared, and what is more important, it is hard to see how any revolutionary situation can recur till the Western end of the war is finished. We had two opportunities, Dunkirk and [the fall of] Singapore, and we took neither. . . . The growing suspicion that we may all have underrated the strength of Capitalism and that the Right may, after all, be able to win the war off its own bat without resorting to any radical change, is very depressing to anyone who thinks. (CW 14, 292)

He did note in the piece that there was enthusiasm for the Beveridge Plan but that no one thought it would be actually adopted. He was right that nothing was done at the time, but it did provide the basis for extremely important social changes after the war. He further reflected on the change in his "London Letter" to the *Partisan Review* that he probably wrote in October 1944.

> I fell into the trap of assuming that "the war and the revolution are inseparable." There were excuses for this belief, but still it was a very great error. For after all, we have not lost the war, unless appearances are very deceiving, and we have not introduced Socialism. Britain is moving towards a planned economy, and class distinctions tend to dwindle, but there has been no real shift of power and no increase in genuine democracy. . . . I over-emphasized the anti-Fascist

character of the war, exaggerated the social changes that were actually occurring; and under-rated the enormous strength of the forces of reaction. (CW 16, 412–414)

The previous April, in a review of a book from the Right, F. A. Hayek's *The Road to Serfdom,* and one from the Left, K. Zilliacus's *The Mirror of the Past*, he put forth the dilemma that would haunt his two most famous books. "Between them these two books sum up our present predicament. Capitalism leads to dole queues, the scramble for markets, and war. Collectivism leads to concentration camps, leader-worship, and war. There is no way out of this unless a planned economy can be somehow combined with the freedom of the intellect, which can only happen if the concept of right and wrong is restored to politics" (CW 16, 150). He did have hope, however, as he wrote in a letter the following May: "I believe very deeply, as I explained in my book 'The Lion and the Unicorn,' in the English *people* and in their capacity to centralise their economy without destroying freedom in doing so." It was in the same letter, perhaps for the first time, that he mentioned his later famous example of the power of the totalitarian state. "If the sort of world that I am afraid of arrives, a world of two or three great superstates which are unable to conquer one another, two and two could become five if the fuhrer wished it" (CW 16, 191). In a column he wrote for the *Manchester Evening News* on March 18, 1945, he had taken a subdued, perhaps resigned, yet optimistic appraisal of what had happened in England itself because of the war. "Without a doubt the general *behaviour* in Britain during the war has been good. All classes have been willing to sacrifice either their lives or their comforts, rationing has been equitable and efficient, profiteering and black-marketing have never been a major problem, industrial production has soared in spite of every kind of difficulty, and women have flung themselves into the war effort to an unprecedented extent" (CW 17, 94). He took a similar tone about the state of the English people during the war in his "London Letter" to the *Partisan Review* in the Summer 1945 issue.

> The ordinary people in the street seem to me not only to have become entirely habituated to a planned, regimented sort of life, in which consumption goods of all kinds are scarce but are shared with reasonable fairness, but actually to prefer it to what they had before. Clearly one can't verify such impressions, but I have believed all along that England has been *happier* during the war, in spite of the desperate tiredness of some periods. . . . In the face of terrifying dangers and golden political opportunities, people just keep on keeping on, in a sort of twilight sleep in which they are conscious of nothing except the daily round of work, family life, darts at the pub, exercising the dog, mowing the lawn, bringing home the supper beer etc., etc. . . . Never would I have prophesied that we could go through nearly six years of war without arriving at either Socialism or Fascism, and with our civil liberties almost intact. I don't know whether this semi-anesthesia in which the British people contrive to live is a sign of decadence, as many observers believe, or whether on the other hand it is a kind of instinctive wisdom. (CW 17, 164–165)

He also wrote a very short book, *The English People*, in late 1943 and early 1944. In many ways it was further testimony to the development of his devotion to his country. He did view it, however, as a piece of propaganda, to provide a sense of what the English were fighting for. The book has an odd history. It was commissioned for the series *Britain in Pictures*, which ultimately consisted of 132 very short books, quite a few by very well-known writers. He signed a contract to write it in September 1943 and had written the text by May 1944. The series was extraordinarily far ranging, with its stated topics covering history, art, social life, natural history, education, religion, literature, science, and country life. As the title *Britain in Pictures* promises, the texts had many illustrations. It encompassed Britain, but Orwell himself only wrote about England, although at times the title of his book was announced as *The British People*.

Lord David Cecil who was a member of the advisory committee on the series recommended against publication after reading Orwell's book. In an undated letter to the editor of the series, W. J. Turner, he wrote: "Orwell's book is not only extremely partisan but also presents England to the foreigner in the most unfavourable light, guilty of all the sins of feudal archaic snobbery of which she is most frequently accused especially in America" (*The Lost Orwell*, 102). Perhaps for that reason, or some others, it wasn't actually published until August 1947. It was one of his most patriotic texts along with *The Lion and the Unicorn* and "My Country Right or Left." It was also one that he did not wish to have reprinted perhaps because he came to regret what might be regarded as his rather sentimental generalizations. Perhaps he did remove some of the text that bothered Cecil, and certainly he revised the text before it was published.

Contrary to Cecil's judgment, its aim was to capture the "ordinary" English person, the vast majority of the country who were working class rather than the upper-class stereotype that foreigners were likely to bring to mind when thinking about England. He wrote that the characteristics of the English common people were "artistic insensibility, gentleness, respect for legality, suspicion of foreigners, sentimentality about animals, hypocrisy, exaggerated class distinctions, and an obsession with sport." It is a characteristic Orwell text, full of powerful generalizations based on his own perceptions of the moment. It is highly unlikely that he had any hard information to back up his perceptive and possibly true assertions. He made some characteristic and important generalizations about how to speak and write. "To write or even to speak English is not a science but an art. There are no reliable rules: there is only the general principle that concrete words are better than abstract ones, and that the shortest way of saying anything is always the best." He also did make some comments on the future of England, that it needed to accept its fate as a secondary power. That was a lesson derived by the course of the war. But he also assumed that it would nevertheless continue somehow to be a "great" power if it could be on good terms with

Russia, Europe, and the United States. He also maintained that there were certain steps necessary in order to preserve a leading role, although it is not clear how England could do so. "These are a rising birthrate, more social equality, less centralisation and more respect for the intellect." On the last topic he remarked, "The English will never develop into a nation of philosophers. They will always prefer instinct to logic, and character to intelligence." And he went on, "England can only fulfill its special mission if the ordinary English in the street can somehow get their hands on power. We were told very frequently during the war years that this time, when the danger was over, there should be no lost opportunities, no recurrence of the past. No more stagnation punctuated by wars, no more Rolls-Royces gliding past dole queues, no return to the England of the Distressed Area" (CW 16, 218–228).

What was Orwell's wartime experience like? He had in fact an extremely busy time, so much so that he did not embark on a major work. The BBC position was very demanding, involving endless correspondence and an extraordinary amount of material he wrote himself: news reports, talks, adaptations of stories by others, and most strikingly, a short story to be written by several authors, including E. M. Forster. There were also the sound magazines, the "London Letters" to the *Partisan Review*, and innumerable book reviews. Living in London was not easy. It was complicated by the Blitz, and in fact the Orwells were bombed out of one of their flats. They moved into several flats in London during this period, and they still spent some time at the cottage in Wallington. Eileen was busy doing war work. Orwell was working very hard at the BBC until he resigned on November 1943. He then took up being the literary editor for the left-wing publication *Tribune* and launched a fine column, "As I Please," on a wide range of subjects. He would continue to comment on the effect that the war was having on English society and how it might have changed but then was reverting to its former state. For example in his column of August 4, 1944, he noted the significance of railings both in private squares and public parks.

> I see that railings are returning—only wooden ones, it is true, but still railings—in one London square after another. So the lawful denizens of the squares can make use of their treasured keys again, and the children of the poor can be kept out. When the railings round the squares and the parks were removed, the object was partly to accumulate scrap iron, but the removal was also felt to be a democratic gesture. Many more green spaces were now open to the public and you could stay in the parks till all hours instead of being hounded out at closing time by grim-faced keepers. (CW 16, 318)

He was no longer a crusader about what changes the war might bring about that had been so much a part of *The Lion and the Unicorn*. As he wrote to John Middleton Murry on August 11, 1944, "There has been very little popular resistance to this war, and also very little hatred. It is a job that needs to be done" (CW 16, 333). Such a view was consistent with his depiction of the population in *The English People*, a rather standard picture of a stoical, understated people.

His salary at *Tribune* was less than he had received at the BBC, but he only needed to work three days a week. Hence he had more time for his own writing, and he was extraordinarily prolific. He wrote some of his most important essays for *Horizon*. He was publishing "London Letters" in the *Partisan Review*. He was doing some writing for *The Observer* and through it becoming a friend of David Astor. He had resigned from the Home Guard at the same time that he left the BBC. He did it on the basis of medical grounds, but indeed these medical issues had always existed and would have served as a reason never to have joined in the first place. He did publicly maintain to a degree his support of the Home Guard in a book review in *The Observer* on May 9, 1943. "Its mere existence—the fact that in the moment of crisis it could be called into being by a few words over the air, the fact that somewhere near two million men have rifles in their bedrooms and the authorities contemplate this without dismay—is a sign of a stability unequalled in any other country in the world" (CW 15, 94). But even so there was no longer a threat of invasion and hence no need for guerilla tactics by a home-based military force. He had in fact become privately disillusioned with the Home Guard almost a year before. As he wrote in his "War-time Diary" on June 21, 1942: "After two years no real training has been done, no specialised tactics worked out, no battle positions fixed upon, no fortifications built—all this owing to endless changing of plan and complete vagueness as to what we are supposed to be aiming at" (CW 13, 367). As a revolution seemed increasingly unlikely, there wouldn't be that possible call upon a domestic military force to fight on its behalf.

He was anxious to have more time for his own writing. He did have a rather busy social life including, apparently, some affairs which Eileen may well have known about. They had agreed to have an open marriage, but other than a probable affair with Georges Kopp in Barcelona there is no indication that she had other lovers. He might well have found the shabbiness of life imposed by the war rather congenial, fitting into the style of life he preferred. It also to some degree brought about a greater appearance of egalitarianism. He and Eileen entertained a fair amount, despite neither of them being in particularly good health. Quite often guests might stay the night on a cot rather than making their way home in a bombed London. Literary life went on, almost in defiance of the war. The culture that one was fighting for must not disappear. In many ways it was for him a highly satisfactory life. He was becoming an increasingly better known and a valued figure in the literary life of England. Through his work at the BBC, primarily arranging talks, he vastly expanded his social circle, particularly with literary figures. Rather oddly, considering his style, he became a patron of others. As literary editor of *Tribune* he was in a position to publish pieces by various authors. He had also been thinking of writing a long family saga. But then

in November 1943 he embarked over the next four months
writing what many regard as his greatest work, *Animal
Farm*. Was it influenced by the war? In some ways, it
seems somewhat strangely removed from the war. Reading it, one has little sense that it was written while a world
war was raging.

The book is related to that rural England evoked to an
extent in *The Lion and the Unicorn* as well as in *Coming
Up for Air*. In many ways the book is a rural fable. Yet at
the same time the events in it are closely based on the
course of the Russian Revolution. He did not necessarily
disapprove of the revolution as such as his major concern
was not Russia itself. He never believed that Communism needed to be overthrown in the Soviet Union, but
he felt very strongly that it should not be imposed on
other countries. He was reacting against what he thought
was the excessive worship of Stalin that he felt was taking
place in England because of Russia's participation in the
war against Hitler. At the same time the story he wished
to tell fit into what he thought was the lesson he learned
from the Spanish Civil War. He had come to be a committed socialist and to believe that it was the best possible
form of government. But at the same time he had become
profoundly pessimistic about its ability to survive as a
system. Those who had brought a potentially good state
into existence inevitably fell in love with power and
would profoundly pervert the revolution in order to
remain in power. They would not be reluctant to take
extreme and very cruel measures in order to preserve

their position. That was the lesson of the Russian Revolution. It was necessary that those in the West should learn it. Of course the irony was that it wasn't very likely that socialist revolutions would take place in the West. But as we have seen, Orwell had felt that a socialist revolution was a necessity in England in order to win the war. He probably realized at the time that he was writing *Animal Farm* that was not going to happen, but it might happen to an extent when the war was won. He certainly admitted that, indeed, as it turned out the radical changes he thought were necessary were not. But that does not mean that his thinking was not profoundly affected by the experience of the war itself. The war was crucial in convincing him of the desirability of the transformation of the state into a socialist one in order to create a better society.

In the preface that he wrote for the Ukrainian edition of *Animal Farm* in 1947, he made totally clear how important the war experience in Spain was for the shaping of that book.

> For the past ten years I have been convinced that the destruction of the Soviet myth was essential if we wanted a revival of the Socialist movement. On my return from Spain I thought of exposing the Soviet myth in a story that could be easily understood by almost everyone and which could be easily translated into other languages. However, the actual details of the story did not come to me for some time until one day (I was then living in a small village) I saw a little boy, perhaps ten years old, driving a huge cart-horse along a

narrow path, whipping it whenever it tried to turn. It struck me that only if such animals became aware of their strength we should have no power over them, and that men exploit animals in much the same way as the rich exploit the proletariat. I proceeded to analyse Marx's theory from the animals' point of view. . . . I did not write it out until 1943, for I was always engaged on other work which gave me no time. . . . Thus the main outlines of the story were in my mind over a period of six years before it was actually written. . . . Although the various episodes are taken from the actual history of the Russian Revolution, they are dealt with schematically and their chronological order is changed; this was necessary for the symmetry of the story. (CW 19, 88–89)

How *Animal Farm* came to be published is a nicely paradoxical tale. The very factors that meant that it took two years to be issued were the same that eventually would help lead to its great commercial success. Of course, it was much assisted by the brilliance of the writing, the creation of a totally believable fable, powerfully told with sharply etched characters, the villainous pigs, particularly Napoleon and Squealer, and the heroic horse Boxer and the cynical donkey Benjamin, among others. Orwell is rather hard on those ordinarily beloved domestic animals, with a morally ambiguous cat and the vicious guard dogs. The manuscript was offered to several publishers. In 1943 the Soviet Union was an essential ally, and to bring out a book that was clearly offensive to that country was hardly helpful for the war effort considering too that the Soviet Union was an ally when the book was finished. In Spain Orwell had been a premature anti-Fascist; now he was a premature anti-Communist.

It took more than a year to find a publisher. Victor Gollancz, who had published all his earlier novels and had edited a collection of essays, *The Betrayal of the Left*, to which Orwell had contributed, about the iniquity of the Nazi-Soviet Pact, was still sufficiently sympathetic to Russia during the war that he refused the book. Orwell did not expect him to accept it, but he was by his contract with Gollancz obligated to offer him first refusal. After all, Russia was still at that moment a stalwart ally, and Stalin had heroic stature. Two further publishers turned it down: Nicholson and Watson and Jonathan Cape even though the latter might have published it if the firm were given an option on future work which still resided with Gollancz. It was also advised by someone in the Ministry of Information not to publish the book. It was discovered later that the person was Peter Smollett, a Soviet spy. Even the conservative T. S. Eliot, with whom Orwell had become quite friendly when he was at the BBC, turned it down. He had arranged for Eliot to give some talks, and they had a few lunches together. He was a principal editor at Faber & Faber, and though he no doubt shared the same views about Russia, he felt he could not publish it while the war was going on and Russia was such an important ally. He rather oddly thought that the pigs were in fact the natural leaders and should have been more public spirited. The publisher William Collins may have turned it down as well. Orwell even

thought of self-publishing it and had the promise of a
loan from David Astor to do so. Eventually Fredric Warburg of Secker and Warburg, who had brought out the
politically unpopular *Homage to Catalonia,* agreed to
publish it. It was perhaps odd that Orwell didn't turn to
Warburg earlier, but he may have wished to use a larger
and better known firm as well as thinking that Warburg
might not like it politically. He also knew that Warburg
was short of paper, a crucial wartime issue. Perhaps
because of the paper question and possibly other concerns, the book wasn't published until August 1945, a year
after it had been accepted. That was some months after
the European war had ended in May and the war with
Japan had just been concluded. By then the attitude
towards Russia in the West was beginning to change
quickly and dramatically. The publication delay meant
that the book stirred up much more positive interest than
it might have otherwise. It was an extraordinary success,
buoyed indeed by its being a powerful argument against
Russia and a very early document of the Cold War. In the
United States, where it appeared the following year, it
was a runaway best seller, buoyed up by being a selection
of the Book-of-the-Month Club, which meant that it
was distributed in the hundreds of thousands. A somewhat known and established writer before its publication, Orwell now was rapidly becoming a world famous
author, a reputation that has become even greater in the
years that followed, based on *Animal Farm* and the subsequent *Nineteen Eighty-Four.*

Animal Farm is in many ways a heartbreaking book. At the very beginning of what might be a truly just and equal society, it breaks down because of selfishness, the pigs keeping back the milk, and then Napoleon's determination to be all powerful. Orwell tells us that he is a socialist and yearns for a just society. But does he believe that it can actually ever happen? Might we have to make do with our deeply flawed capitalist yet, to an extent, democratic society? Might Winston Churchill's remark that democracy was a terrible system but that it is better than any other have a certain validity? There is the poignant moment when the horse Clover is in despair over the execution of fellow animals: the purges.

> As Clover looked down the hillside her eyes filled with tears. If she could have spoken her thoughts, it would have been to say that this was not what they had aimed at when they set themselves years ago to work for the overthrow of the human race. These scenes of terror and slaughter were not what they had looked forward to on that night when old Major first stirred them to rebellion. If she herself had had any picture of the future, it had been of a society of animals set free from hunger and the whip, all equal, each working according to his capacity, the strong protecting the weak, as she had protected the lost brood of ducklings with her foreleg on the night of Major's speech. (CW 8, 58)

Orwell saw as the only hope the "people" turning on their power-mad rulers. How realistic a solution that is is another matter. As he wrote to Dwight Macdonald, the American political essayist and Orwell's publisher at the

Partisan Review, about the book in December 1946: "Of course I intended it primarily as a satire on the Russian revolution. But I did mean it to have a wider application in so much that I meant that *that kind* of revolution (violent conspiratorial revolution, led by unconsciously power-hungry people) can only lead to a change of masters. I meant the moral to be that revolutions only effect a radical improvement when the masses are alert and know how to chuck out their leaders as soon as the latter have done their job" (CW 18, 507). On the other hand, the book was taken as being much more virulently anti-Communist than even Orwell intended. In a sense that was unavoidable with the pigs being so detestable. He didn't wish for the Soviet Union itself to be destroyed but rather its myth. He was pointing out as well, with *Animal Farm*, how the story of the Russian Revolution also vividly demonstrated how socialism could go wrong. He remained deeply committed to the ultimate aim of achieving some sort of a democratic socialist state. Indeed in the unlikely event that such a state came into existence, it might even provide a model for the Soviet Union to reform itself. Most importantly he stated, "*Animal Farm* was the first book in which I tried, with full consciousness of what I was doing, to fuse political purpose and artistic purpose into one whole" (CW 18, 320). In a sense it was parallel to the fusion he had achieved both during and because of the war itself of socialism and patriotism in its particular English form. Here the very brief ideal society locates itself in the countryside despite the fact that so much of England was urban. Paradoxically he provided material both for hopeful socialists and convinced anti-socialists. At the same time he remained deeply pessimistic that a socialist revolution could ultimately succeed. As he wrote in an unpublished essay on Arthur Koestler in September 1944, "All revolutions are failures, but they are not all the same failure" (CW 16, 400). But that did not mean that he did not hope that some form of socialism might be achieved, as extremely difficult and unlikely as that might be.

Much of the impetus for *Nineteen Eighty-Four* arose out of a society that was at war. Orwell's take on the state of the war also provided a picture of what he saw as a possible future for the world. As he wrote in one of his "As I Please" columns for *Tribune* on February 2, 1945:

> Germany, I suppose, will be defeated this year, and when Germany is out of the war Japan will not be able to stand up to the combined power of Britain and the U.S.A. Then there will be a peace of exhaustion, with only minor and unofficial wars raging all over the place, and perhaps this so-called peace may last for decades. But after that, by the way the world is actually shaping, it may well be that war will *become permanent*. Already, quite visibly and more or less with the acquiescence of all of us, the world is splitting up into two or three huge super-states. . . . It is likely that these vast states will be permanently at war with one another. (CW 17, 38–39)

Now that the war was drawing to a close and he had finished writing *Animal Farm*, he was anxious to see the last days of the war firsthand. Despite his bad health and his new obligations as the father of an adopted boy, he resigned from his position at *Tribune* and became a war correspondent for *The Observer*. He was off to France and Germany. That trip was tragically interrupted by the sudden death of his wife Eileen on March 29, 1945, during an operation that was not expected to be life threatening. With an adopted son to care for on his own and the ideas of *Nineteen Eighty-Four* bubbling in his mind, his health not at all good, his life was very complicated. He was able to secure the help of Susan Watson to look after his son, Richard, and he would propose to several young women in the years to come to assist him with his son, to provide love, with the implied promise to be a well-off literary widow in the not too distant future.

5 THE COLD WAR

In the sadly brief five years that he had to live, Orwell's greatest accomplishment and a major cause for his enduring fame was the writing of *Nineteen Eighty-Four*. With his declining health, it was a slow process. Although in London for some months, in the years after the war he spent much of his time in a remote house, Barnhill, on the island of Jura in the Inner Hebrides. He did have quite a few visitors there, but its remoteness was emphasized by the elaborate instructions he sent to them about how to get to him on a two-day trip by train, boat, car, and the last bit generally on foot. As a place to write it was not ideal, and he failed in his attempt to employ even briefly a secretary there. He did love the opportunity to garden, both vegetable and decorative, and to fish. He was also involved in a near fatal accident when he was on a boating excursion with his son and two of the older children of his sister Marjorie, who had recently died. They were caught in the Corryvreckan whirlpool, the third largest in the world. He also spent quite a bit of time in sanatoriums trying to cope with his tuberculosis, first near Edinburgh and later in the Cotswolds before spending his last weeks in University College Hospital in London. Susan Watson came to help him with his son, Richard. His sister Avril was also there to assist, but she and Susan didn't get on and Susan left. Bill Dunn also came to help with the farm work, and some years later in 1951 he married Avril.

Nineteen Eighty-Four became a Cold War classic, demonstrating the evils of the Soviet system. It was less tightly modeled on the history of Russia since its revolution than *Animal Farm,* but it clearly derived a significant part of its content from the parallels between Big Brother and Stalin and the control of people's minds that was part of the Soviet world. This led many to believe, wrongly in my view, that Orwell was anti-socialist. When *Animal Farm* was so construed in the United States, he had to issue a specific denial affirming his commitment to socialism and his support of the Labour Party.

The final "war" that he would participate in, be influenced by, and made crucial contributions to shaping was the Cold War. *Animal Farm* and *Nineteen Eighty-Four,* whatever else they might be, were undoubtedly documents of the Cold War. It cannot be sufficiently emphasized that Orwell held the perhaps unusual position of being a Cold War socialist. There were of course many anti-Communist socialists, particularly after Hungary and Khrushchev's speech denouncing Stalin in 1956. But

I believe to be a Cold War socialist was comparatively rare, not quite the same thing as being an anti-Communist socialist. It meant he was far more willing than others to support the Cold War and to be active in doing so. Primarily because of that, the ways his work has been used, but also in some cases what he actually wrote, has attracted some very strong criticism from the Left, as in such collections as *Inside the Myth: Orwell: Views from the Left*, edited by Christopher Norris and brought out by the Communist publisher, Lawrence and Wishart, in 1984. There is a continual debate between those who think of Orwell as a figure of the Left, the dominant view, and to my way of thinking the correct one, and those who would prefer him to be rightwards leaning or at least inadvertently supporting the Right. Ironically it is rather similar to the argument he had made about pacifists, that in effect they were supporting Fascism. Those on the Right would like to see his two most famous works as giving considerable support to the idea that socialism is a bad idea. Those on the Left believe that he argued that socialism was a good idea and should come about, but it would be in great danger of almost inevitably disintegrating and becoming a totalitarian regime because of the obsession of the leaders of the revolution to maintain their power. The only solution he visualized was if there was to be a continual and frequent change of those in power. Perhaps that is a major factor in democracies being preserved, the use of elections, if they are not corrupted, resulting in changing leadership. There is no

question that the novels, based as they are on the history
of the Soviet Union, were deeply influential Cold War
documents on the side of the West. Indeed the reissue of
Homage to Catalonia in 1952 and its growing popularity
were in good part because of its anti-Soviet position. So
too *Animal Farm* and *Nineteen Eighty-Four* owed quite a
bit of their popularity to their being anti-Soviet works.
This does not account, however, for the current great
popularity of *Nineteen Eighty-Four*; although it had
always sold well, it now sells even more widely, triggered
by the rise of the surveillance state and the presidency of
Donald Trump having made us increasingly conscious
of "fake news" and "alternative facts." Within four days
of Kellyanne Conway, counselor to Trump, using the
latter phrase, sales of *Nineteen Eighty-Four* went up
9,500 percent.

Despite the books being Cold War documents it
always must be remembered, as Orwell wrote in a letter
in November 1945: "I belong to the Left and must work
inside it, much as I hate Russian totalitarianism" (CW 17,
385). He was irritated that particularly in the United
States some took the book as an attack on socialism and
on the Labour Party itself. He issued a statement in June
1949 that was published in several American outlets. "My
novel *Nineteen Eighty-four* is *not* intended as an attack on
socialism or on the British Labor party, but as a show-up
of the perversions to which a centralized economy is liable, and which have already been partly realized in Communism and fascism" (CW 20, 135).

What is frequently not noted is that George Orwell was, apparently, the first recorded coiner of the term *Cold War*. This was the last "war" after the First World War, the Spanish Civil War, and the Second World War that was deeply influential in shaping him. His use of the phrase appeared in an essay "You and the Atom Bomb," published on October 19, 1945, in *Tribune* where he would write an occasional column after his resignation as its literary editor. In this one he discussed, in a very imaginative way, the political implications of weapons: "I think the following rule would be found generally true: that ages in which the dominant weapon is expensive or difficult to make will tend to be ages of despotism, whereas when the dominant weapon is cheap and simple, the common people have a chance. Thus, for example, tanks, battleships and bombing planes are inherently tyrannical weapons, while rifles, muskets, longbows and hand grenades are inherently democratic weapons." Now with the United States having the atomic bomb and the Soviet Union likely to have it in the very near future, Orwell predicted that it would create a situation in which the two contending states would survive because of their possession of atomic weapons: "A State that is at once *unconquerable* and in a permanent state of 'cold war' with its neighbours . . . prolonging indefinitely 'a peace that is no peace'" (CW 17, 319–321). Bernard Baruch, the American financier and political adviser, is often credited for coining the phrase in April 1947, and the American columnist Walter Lipmann for giving it wider circulation in his 1947 book, *The Cold War: A Study of U.S. Foreign Policy*. Yet, according to the *Oxford English Dictionary*, Orwell is the first cited person to use the term to describe the relation between the West and the Soviet Union, and ultimately it became common usage. He might have had rather mixed feelings about the success of the term. One of his most important language causes was to teach us that we should avoid catchphrases that were likely to block the way to clear thinking. It is rather striking that it was in 1945 that he wrote one of his most famous essays dealing with such questions, "Politics and the English Language."

There is no question that, shaped by his legitimate hatred of the Soviet Union and in what he saw, correctly, as its perversion of socialism, he became virulently anti-Communist. What is striking about him and I think is too easily forgotten was that though he can be seen as a Cold War warrior he was also a Cold War socialist. Because of his Spanish Civil War experiences he was both a premature anti-Fascist and a premature "Cold Warrior." He had seen how despicably the Russians had acted in Spain. He had written against the hypocrisy of the Soviet-Nazi pact. He became a rather paradoxical Cold Warrior. I think it is accurate to say that most Cold Warriors saw the Cold War as a conflict between capitalism and socialism. They might recognize that socialism as practiced in the Soviet Union had deviated in many ways from its original ideas, but they nevertheless believed that capitalism rather than socialism was the much preferred political system. Orwell, of course, argued in *Animal Farm* and would demonstrate in *Nineteen Eighty-Four* even more power-fully how socialism could be easily perverted and lead to a totalitarian government. He became a very rare Cold War socialist. Contrary to his intentions he did provide, how-ever, what many took as powerful arguments against socialism itself and what they believed would be the inevi-table course it would take. As he stated some years later, "Destruction of the Soviet myth was essential if we wanted a revival of the Socialist movement" (CW 19, 88).

Even before the war in Europe was ending in the Spring of 1945, it was clear that there was likely to be future antagonism, perhaps even war, between the Soviet Union and the West. Given Orwell's values and his staunch anti-Communism, one might think he would not regard this as necessarily a bad thing. Yet he had never really advocated the destruction of the Soviet Union even though he thought that "the existing Russian régime is a mainly evil thing" (CW 17, 259). In a piece for *The Observer* on May 27, 1945, in a discussion of possible joint rule in Germany and Austria, he wrote, "Certain dangerous illusions—for instance, the widespread idea that the U.S.S.R. and the Western Powers will be at war in the near future—have sprung up and need to be con-tradicted by the highest authorities" (CW 17, 161).

In terms of what was happening domestically, his reaction to the British General Election of July 1945 was consistent with his subdued expectation of the future in contrast to his earlier hope that there would be revolu-tionary change in Britain. He had predicted wrongly that there might be a narrow Labour victory rather than its extraordinary electoral triumph, resulting in the party's great majority in Parliament that made possible the creation of a welfare state. In his "London Letter" for the *Partisan Review* he wrote that summer, he was modest in his expectations. "One cannot take this slide to the Left as meaning that Britain is on the verge of revolution. In spite of the discontent smoldering in the armed forces, the mood of the country seems to me to be less revolutionary, less Utopian, even less hopeful, than it was in 1940 or 1942. . . . The great need of the moment is to make people aware of what is happening and why, and to persuade them that Socialism is a *better* way of life but not necessarily, in its first stages, a more comfortable one" (CW 17, 246–248). He made his subdued expectations even clearer in a piece he wrote for the American Jewish publication *Commentary* published in November. "A Labor government will approach such problems as the occupation of Germany with more common sense than has been shown hitherto, it will look with a friendlier eye on the Italian Socialists and the Spanish Republicans, and it will go somewhat further towards satisfying Jewish aspirations in Palestine: but Britain's strategic interests, in a world of competing nationalisms, remain the same, whether the government at home is called Socialist or capitalist" (CW 17, 340).

By 1946 he was profoundly pessimistic about the future and what might happen in the world, thinking that obviously very much shaped *Nineteen Eighty-Four*.

As he wrote in an "As I Please" column in *Tribune* on November 29:

> When one considers how things have gone since 1930 or thereabouts, it is not easy to believe in the survival of civilisation. I do not argue from this that the only thing to do is to abjure practical politics, retire to some remote place and concentrate either on individual salvation or on building up self-supporting communities against the day when the atom bombs have done their work. I think one must continue the political struggle, just as a doctor must try to save the life of a patient who is probably going to die. . . . It is not easy to find a direct economic explanation of the behaviour of the people who now rule the world. The desire for pure power seems to be much more dominant that the desire for wealth. (CW 18, 503–504)

By the summer of 1947, in a piece he wrote for the *Partisan Review,* his prediction for the future was also bleak. He felt it was possible that the United States would use the atomic bomb against Russia before Russia had one, but he thought this was unlikely. A second alternative envisioned the Cold War being terminated by a hot war. "The present 'cold war' will continue until the USSR, and several other countries, have atomic bombs as well. Then there will only be a short breathing-space before whizz! go the rockets, wallop! go the bombs, and the industrial centers of the world are wiped out, probably beyond repair." This would result not in socialism but the survival of society at a primitive level. The third alternative prefiguring what he was writing in *Nineteen Eighty-Four* he saw as the worst. Though the powers would refrain from using the atomic bomb, nevertheless there would be a "division of the world among two or three vast superstates, unable to conquer one another and unable to be overthrown by an internal rebellion. In all probability their structure would be hierarchic, with a semidivine caste at the top and out-right slavery at the bottom, and the crushing out of liberty would exceed anything the world had yet seen. . . . Civilizations of this type might remain static for thousands of years." Despite all this gloom, he still felt that what he called democratic socialism might avoid these scenarios. But in a rather patronizing way he wrote that only in Western Europe, as well as in Australia and New Zealand, was there sufficient sympathy for socialism that it might be achieved. The United States was too committed to capitalism and its materialism. "Therefore a socialist United States of Europe seems to me the only worth-while political objective today." (He later thought it might be Western Europe plus Africa.) He concluded this somewhat grim analysis with a sliver of hope. "It is even possible that if the world falls apart into three unconquerable superstates, the liberal tradition will be strong enough within the Anglo-American section of the world to make life tolerable and even offer some hope of progress. But all this is speculation. The actual lookout, so far as I can calculate the probabilities, is very dark, and any serious thought should start out from that fact" (CW 19, 163–167). He did state some months later in a piece that was never published, probably written in the summer of 1947, that "we are no longer strong enough to stand alone, and if we fail to bring a western European Union into being, we shall be obliged, in the long run, to subordinate our policy to that of one Great Power or the other. And in spite of all the fashionable chatter of the moment, everyone knows in his heart that we should choose America" (CW 19, 182). A year later he somewhat contradicted this view. Orwell changed his mind quite often, but he did so with such authority that he gave one the sense that he had always held the view that he was now stating. Here he is commenting on what he felt was the real possibility that Britain would become part of the United States, which he condemns with perhaps a rather surprising generalization. "It is unacceptable from a British point of view since it would mean becoming very definitely a junior partner and being tied to a country which everyone except a few Tories regards as politically backward" (CW 19, 437).

Pessimism did not totally overwhelm him as is evident at the end of his wonderful essay "Some Thoughts on the Common Toad" with its sense of some hope. Life and nature would persist. Living so much in his last years on Jura in the Hebrides kept him in touch with those forces. "The atom bombs are piling up in the factories, the police are prowling through the cities, the lies are streaming from the loudspeakers, but the earth is still going round the sun, and neither the dictators nor the bureaucrats, deeply as they disapprove of the process, are able to prevent it" (CW 18, 240).

Nineteen Eighty-Four became probably the single most important cultural document of the Cold War and has continued to be widely read. It has enjoyed an ever increasing popularity in recent years not so much now from its Cold War aspects but more because of Orwell's uncanny ability to have predicted the ever increasing degree that we live in a surveillance state and how easily "facts" about the past and indeed the present can be changed through the great and growing power of computers. The life depicted in its pages is extreme in its horror, but it does show what totalitarianism either of the Right or the Left might well become. Unlike at the beginning of *Animal Farm,* in *Nineteen Eighty-Four* there is no conception that once there was a more just and equal society, although even at the beginning of *Animal Farm* the pigs are hoarding the milk. We are not told what the principles of "Ingsoc" are that presumably shaped the beginning of this world after the conclusion of the Second World War. The vast majority of the population are the "proles" who seem to be in survival mode. There is some hope that they might rebel and they do maintain some inner spirit, leading their own not totally cheerless lives. But there is little indication in the main text that a successful rebellion of the proles is likely to come about. There are the rulers, the Inner Party, the managers, who have both power and a high level of living. Their sole purpose is to maintain that power. There is the tightly controlled Outer Party, in effect the servants of the Inner Party who, heavily supervised, do the task of revising the past, organizing the Two Minute Hates, and executing in other ways how the country is controlled. There is continual warfare going on against one of the two other world states, Eurasia or Eastasia, although that may be switched at the same time that it is asserted that there has never been a change. But we are never told any details about the fighting. This is very much an oppressive domestic story, taking place in the rooms of the Ministry of Truth where history is changed and in the Ministry of Love, a prison where the ultimate personalized torture is delivered in Room 101. There is also the space supervised by telescreens where members of the Outer Party live and as it turns out the spied upon love nest of Winston and Julia.

There are I believe, however, several crucial ambiguities in *Nineteen Eighty-Four* that provide some possible glimmers of hope that this totalitarian state will eventually be undermined, despite the deeply pessimistic ending of the novel itself: "He loved Big Brother." Might this totalitarian society be overthrown or undermined through the proletariat? Was there hope in the proles? That possibility might be represented by the woman heard lustily singing by Winston and Julia from their love nest. On the other hand, that sliver of hope happens just before Winston and Julia are arrested—does that mean that change will never take place? There is also the possibility raised that this totalitarian society might have fallen on some date after 1984. The Appendix on the nature of Newspeak suggests this. It is written in the past tense suggesting that Oceania no longer exists. But it is far from clear that Newspeak and its associated totalitarian state have actually fallen. There are no indications of what may have replaced it and what is the present state of Airstrip One.

The more immediate issue in the few months that remained in Orwell's life between the publication of *Nineteen Eighty-Four* and his death was the interpretation, particularly strong in the United States, that it was written from the politically right point of view against any form of a socialist society, which he refuted. Ironically, *Nineteen Eighty-Four* might be seen as an anti–Cold War document. Fighting the Cold War might lead the West in its turn to become more totalitarian. On the other hand, he would have been unlikely to have written either *Animal Farm* or *Nineteen Eighty-Four* if he had not wanted passionately to portray what was happening in the Soviet Union as representing a very serious danger of what might happen in the West. It must be emphasized, contrary to what some may have thought, that he was not advocating the destruction of the Soviet Union itself but rather that its model of a totalitarian state must not be reproduced elsewhere. To lessen that possibility in his beloved England was central in making him a Cold War patriot.

For his American audience he wrote this powerful statement about his book in the extremely popular magazine, *Life*, on July 25, 1949:

> It has been suggested by some of the reviewers of NINE-TEEN EIGHTY-FOUR that it is the author's view that this, or something like this, is what will happen inside the next

forty years in the Western world. This is not correct. I think that, allowing for the book being after all a parody, something like NINETEEN EIGHTY-FOUR *could* happen. This is the direction in which the world is going at the present time, and the trend lies deep in the political, social and economic foundations of the contemporary world situation.

Specifically the danger lies in the structure imposed on Socialist and on Liberal capitalist communities by the necessity to prepare for total war with the U.S.S.R. and the new weapons, of which of course the atomic bomb is the most powerful and the most publicized. But danger lies also in the acceptance of a totalitarian outlook by intellectuals of all colours.

The moral to be drawn from this dangerous nightmare situation is a simple one: *Don't let it happen. It depends on you.* (CW 20, 134)

A few days later on July 31 a further comment by him was published in the *New York Times Book Review* quoting from a letter Orwell had written to a member of the United Automobile Workers union. "My recent novel is *not* intended as an attack on socialism or on the British Labor party (of which I am a supporter) but as a show-up of the perversions to which a centralized economy is liable and which have already been partly realized in communism and fascism" (CW 20, 135).

Why did *Nineteen Eighty-Four* become such an important Cold War document? And so extraordinarily successful along with *Animal Farm*? By 1989 the two books had been translated into sixty languages and had sold forty million copies (Louis Menand, *The Free World: Art and Thought in the Cold War,* New York: Picador, 2021, 38). They were certainly profoundly anti-Russian and anti-Communist, but they did not advocate the actual destruction of the Soviet state. *Nineteen Eighty-Four* projected a future world that had not come into existence yet and was unlikely to do so in reality. Though as I've mentioned, it did turn out to be predictive about the growth of the surveillance state and the power of computers. The concept of Big Brother undoubtedly played a part in its popularity with its similarity to how Stalin was characterized as Uncle Joe during the war. In Britain and Europe, but not in the United States, it caught to a degree the austerity of life in the immediate postwar years as well as what life was like during the war itself. It took what totalitarianism could become to its ultimate extreme based to a considerable degree on the Soviet state. To its readers during the Cold War it provided a vision of what must be fought against and the need to emphasize, in effect, what were the virtues of the "free" world, ideally an ability to live a free life, certainly to think as one might wish, and to act, within reason, as one might wish. With the destruction of Nazi Germany, the Soviet Union and its satellites and China remained as totalitarian societies, so neatly capsulated as the two other empires in the book.

Nineteen Eighty-Four has great power, perennial popularity, and extraordinary spikes in sales when public events seem to echo it, such as the Edward Snowden revelations and events in the Trump administration. (Ironically, supporters of Trump, such as his son and Josh Hawley, accuse their opponents of "Orwellian" tactics.) Its extraordinary appeal and its continuing popularity can also be attributed to its ability to attract such a wide range of readers. It is an exciting and grim story. It can also reinforce the views of so many no matter where they may be on the political spectrum. For those on the Left it argues how vigilant a socialist society needs to be in order for it not, as in the Soviet Union, to become totalitarian. For those on the Right, whatever Orwell's intentions, it demonstrated the need to fight the Soviet Union in the Cold War. It was necessary for those readers to be sure that there was not sufficient appeal to those in the West for some sort of socialism that would inevitably, in their view, lead to the world that was depicted in *Nineteen Eighty-Four*. As in the statement quoted above, Orwell tried to control how his work was interpreted. As he died just a few months after it was published, he could no longer have an influence upon on how it was viewed. In any case the book profoundly affected the way in which so many of its readers perceived what was at stake in the Cold War. Extreme as its vision was of what might happen not only in the Soviet Union if the Cold War was lost, a driving force for Orwell was his profound love of his own country and his fear that it might transform itself into Airstrip One. In any case it was a runaway best seller, helped in the United States by being a selection of the extremely popular Book-of-the-Month Club.

In many ways one of the most vivid examples of the combination of his intense patriotism while not losing his commitment to socialism is the vexed issue of the list of fellow travelers and crypto-Communists that he compiled in the spring of 1949 while very ill and just months before his death. He enjoyed making lists—for instance some years before he had speculated on who might support the Nazis if Britain were invaded and conquered. He now provided a list to the government of those he thought might be appropriate to ask to write pieces for various publications in support of the West. But then sometime later he provided a further list of those to avoid. In it he provided the names of various individuals that he felt should not be asked to write anything ostensibly to support the West. Most of them were very unlikely to be asked to do so in any case. Orwell was aware of that. The list presents, I believe, an issue for Orwell admirers such as myself and has been the subject of much debate, with a fair number of those on the Left attacking Orwell for compiling such a list. A commitment frequently associated with Orwell is his belief in the importance of human decency. Is compiling such a list, in fact a black list, consistent with human decency? For many of his admirers, particularly on the Right, the overriding commitment to fight the totalitarian state as it was found in the Soviet Union was a total justification. For others, on the Left, it was a betrayal of the values that Orwell claimed to hold. But he was not always consistent in his beliefs. Potentially his list could cause harm to the individuals mentioned, but there is no evidence that it actually did so. Does that excuse him? Was compiling the list actually so bad? Perhaps so. It did upset many when its existence was revealed in 1996. Did his illness cloud his judgment? Perhaps.

How did the list come about? The crucial figure is his friend the beautiful Celia Kirwan, a prominent debutante in her time. She was the twin sister of Arthur Koestler's wife; Orwell had met her at the Koestlers in 1945. She was one of the young women whom he liked and had approached after the tragic death of his wife in the hopes of an affair or even better a marriage which would provide him with companionship, affection, and help with the raising of his adopted son Richard. She was fond of him and very fond of Richard but had no interest in marrying him or having an affair. During a visit to the Koestlers in Wales, along with Richard, she was rather struck by his reply when asked what quality he would like to have if he could choose one. He said he would like to be irresistible to women. Although she did resist him, they remained friends and they kept in touch. Sometime later she went to work in Paris for the magazine *Occident*. In February 1949 she wrote to him that she was back in England. That March she came to see him in the sanatorium where he was staying in the Cotswolds in order to solicit his help. She had a position at the Information Research Department, an important agency at the Foreign Office. It had been established by the Labour Foreign Secretary, Ernest Bevin, in January 1948 and approved by the Labour Cabinet. Orwell's good friends, Arthur Koestler and Malcolm Muggeridge, were advisers to the agency. It was not totally secret, although it could receive funds without Parliamentary approval and was not subject to Parliamentary supervision. It was quite large, consisting of four to five hundred individuals, and was dedicated to fighting the Cold War. At this point the Information Research Department was beginning to pursue the strategy of establishing covert publishing activity in support of anti-Communist activity in the Cold War. It was actively involved, but not publicly, in making *Animal Farm* better known around the world. In November 1949 it helped arrange the translation of *Nineteen Eighty-Four* into eighteen different languages (Paul Lashmar and James Oliver, *Britain's Secret Propaganda War,* London: Sutton, 1998, 96). In theory Britain might represent a third way, neither capitalism nor Communism, but the anti-capitalist position didn't appear to play much of a part in its activities. One of its missions was supporting writers and publications financially and secretly so they might in their work combat Russian totalitarianism and the USSR in general. Its original commitment was to extol the virtues of the West through covertly supporting writers who would do so. Quite rapidly it became very active. It was fighting against the considerable Soviet efforts to fight the cultural Cold War. It continued until the agency was closed down in 1977. Ironically one of the publications it supported, secretly, was *Tribune*. Ideally those who received its support should have somewhat left-wing credentials which would give their anti-Russian statements more credibility. It also subsidized quite a few books that put the case for the West, notably several titles by Bertrand Russell. In the years to come it would arrange for and pay for editions of *Animal Farm* in many languages. But it is unclear how much it actually did in placing pieces by particular writers —perhaps a great deal. The Orwell list is controversial in terms of evaluating him. But in looking at it in some detail, it is fairly obvious that virtually no one on it would actually be subsidized to write anti-Soviet pieces as quite a few of them were well known, with some exceptions, to take a sympathetic view of the Soviet Union.

The work of the Information Research Department was divided into two categories: acquiring relevant intelligence gathered by other agencies as well as other parts of the Foreign Office and preparing relevant briefings to be sent to the media, academics, trade union leaders, and foreign officials. It was interested in recruiting staff who had wartime experience in propaganda as well as East European émigrés. Among its eight permanent officials at the time was Robert Conquest (who would write an admiring poem about Orwell) and the Soviet spy Guy Burgess. (See W. Scott Lucas and C. J. Morris, "A Very British Crusade: The Information Research Department and the Beginning of the Cold War," *British Intelligence, Strategy and the Cold War, 1945–51,* ed. Richard J. Aldrich, London: Routledge, 1992.) Celia Kirwan shared an office with Conquest at the agency (he wrote a poem admiring her beauty), and he much approved of Orwell's actions in helping the agency. It seems unlikely that any of the people Orwell listed were approached other than possibly Stephen Spender who played a considerable role in the Cold War. He was in fact quite helpful to the side of the West despite Orwell warning the government against him. But it would obviously be an issue how to avoid those who were in fact pro-Russian, although Orwell's advice was unlikely to have played any significant role. One fears that it was an ineffectual act that in the view of quite a few had done Orwell's reputation no good. I'm not at all sure how I myself feel about it. There is something nasty about besmirching individuals behind their backs. And yet he wanted to do all he could to fight the Communists, although he was against outlawing the Party in Britain and he never believed that the Soviet state should be toppled. His object was to prevent to the extent he could the West becoming enamored by the Communist system and wishing to move in that direction, and to make it clear to others the inequities of the Soviet world without losing his commitment to socialism. The operations of the Information Research Department were not the same as the less benign operations of the CIA, although it certainly veered in that direction. Anything more deeply involving spies and regime change would be within the purview of MI6. The primary mission of the Information Research Department was to wage the cultural Cold War. Orwell had already made a highly significant contribution to that cause through *Animal Farm,* and he was about to publish his newest book. As a result of the first visit with Celia Kirwan, at her wish he suggested some anti-Communist names of those he felt might write effectively for the agency.

She was also looking for a publisher who might, with a secret subsidy, be willing to publish anti-Communist books. Orwell rather surprisingly suggested Victor Gollancz who now, though no longer enthusiastic about Russia, would be unlikely to accept secret money. But he said that Gollancz was now too preoccupied with questions of Palestinian dispossession to be interested, and he would try to think of another publisher (Lashmar, 96–97). One is surprised that he thought he was on sufficiently good terms with Gollancz to approach him about the possibility. Kirwan wrote a memo after her visit to him for the agency, providing a few names of those he thought should write pieces, such as Franz Borkenau whose book on Spain Orwell had publicly praised (CW 20, 319–321). The ideal writer was someone who was seen as being on the Left, and so the anti-Soviet opinions expressed would carry greater weight. But would such writers be willing to accept material and possibly also payment secretly supplied by a government agency? But they might not know that the government was the source of the money as it would come via a particular publication. That question did not appear to have come up. Subsequent to their meeting, Orwell wrote to Kirwan on April 6 with names that he approved of. In that letter he offered to provide a list of those he thought shouldn't be asked. It was very clear that he realized that these individuals were to be used as "propagandists." As he wrote: "I could also, if it is of any value, give you a list of journalists & writers who in my opinion are crypto-Communists, fellow-travellers or inclined that way & should not be trusted as propagandists. But for that I shall have to send for a notebook which I have at home, & I if do give you such a list it is strictly confidential, as I imagine it is libelous to describe somebody as a fellow-traveller" (CW 20, 322). She replied that she would be very happy to have such a list. Sometime later he sent her a list of thirty-eight names of those characterized as crypto-Communists or fellow travelers who were to be avoided. He sent the list from the sanatorium on May 2. It was written at the height of the Cold War, just after the Berlin airlift had ended. In it he said about the list: "It isn't very sensational and I don't suppose it will tell your friends anything they don't know. . . . Even as it stands I imagine that this list is very libellous, or slanderous, or whatever the term is, so will you please see to it that it is returned to me without fail"(CW 20, 103).

Over the course of the 1990s gradually more and more information became known about Orwell's notorious list, causing a considerable controversy about his character. There were innumerable press articles as news of the list became better known in 1996 and again in 1998. The pieces were divided: either defending Orwell generally from the Right and attacking him generally from the Left. His original list which Richard Rees retrieved for him from Barnhill had 135 names all given in Peter Davison's Orwell edition (CW 20, 242–259). That apparently was also sent to the Information Research Department where it was copied and returned although the short annotated list wasn't. *Nineteen Eighty-Four,* published not long after, was his most significant public action as a socialist Cold Warrior. The making of the list was a significant private action and raised the question of what was legitimate in supporting the fight against the Soviet Union as a totalitarian state. It also made clear how difficult it might be to be a patriotic socialist.

Perhaps it is appropriate that Orwell's almost last "wartime" action—other than of course the publication of *Nineteen Eighty-Four* itself—should have this rather ambiguous aspect to it. It also demonstrates how many of his actions and reactions were shaped by wartime issues, although the last war he participated in was not a hot war. It might have become one. What I have tried to demonstrate in this short text is how influenced Orwell was by wartime events, how important they were in shaping his thoughts and writings and making him such an intense patriotic socialist. His patriotism came out of his background, class position, and his education. Being at St. Cyprian's and Eton in the years leading up to the First World and during the war itself helped hone his skills to write so effectively in his criticism of his society. He knew its power structure from within. The Spanish Civil War had completed his commitment to socialism but also made him acutely aware of how it could be threatened and undermined. The Second World War, with England so endangered, reinforced his love for his country but also convinced him that it would be at its best if it were a socialist society. The Cold War made him even more acutely aware of the evils of totalitarianism. All of these experiences were central in creating the great and important writer that he became as well as both a patriot and a socialist. He made writing about politics and other subjects into an art and left us one of the most glorious intellectual and literary legacies of the modern age.

ACKNOWLEDGMENTS

Over the many years I've been thinking and writing about Orwell I've incurred debts to individuals too many to mention. They have made contributions to this short book through their writings, exchanges by letter and emails, and too few meetings in person. There has been the delight of getting to know Dione Venables in connection with the founding of the Orwell Society. Now more recently there have been talks organized by the society. Through Zoom it has been possible for those interested to attend them from all over the world, hear the latest thoughts about Orwell, and have the pleasure of seeing and hearing not only the fellow attendees but the events' presiding figures: Richard Blair and Quentin Kopp. I've benefited greatly through correspondence with that meticulous Orwell scholar, Darcy Moore. I also must mention John Rodden and Christopher Angel. I am deeply grateful to Margo Irvin and her colleagues at the Stanford University Press for their great skill in making it possible for this book to come into existence.

But my most important debt is to the preeminent Orwell scholar I've never met: Peter Davison, the editor of the twenty-volume *The Complete Works of George Orwell* (London: Secker & Warburg, 1998), the first nine volumes being Orwell's full-length books. In the further eleven volumes can be found all that was known at the time of publication of his voluminous other writings ranging from short books, innumerable articles, columns and reviews in periodicals and elsewhere, his diary, poems, and letters. There is also, edited by Peter Davison, a supplemental volume, *The Lost Orwell* (London: Timewell Press, 2006). All entries are accompanied by extremely helpful notes. Virtually all the quotations in my text are from these volumes, and I am so grateful to them. Orwell's words are short selections from different texts and are either out of copyright or are published as "fair usage."